DON'T QUIT
IN THE PIT

Power to turn
any situation around!

DANETTE JOY CRAWFORD

WHITAKER
HOUSE

Unless otherwise indicated, all Scripture quotations are taken from the *Holy Bible, New International Version*`, NIV`, © 1973, 1978, 1984 by the International Bible Society. Used by permission of Zondervan. All rights reserved. Scripture quotations marked (NKJV) are taken from the *New King James Version*, © 1979, 1980, 1982, 1984 by Thomas Nelson, Inc. Used by permission. All rights reserved. Scripture quotations marked (AMP) are taken from the *Amplified* Bible, © 1954, 1958, 1962, 1964, 1965, 1987 by The Lockman Foundation. Used by permission. (www.Lockman.org)

Unless otherwise indicated, all word definitions are taken from
Merriam-Webster's 11th Collegiate Dictionary.

DON'T QUIT IN THE PIT:
Power to Turn Any Situation Around!

Danette Joy Crawford
P.O. Box 65036
Virginia Beach, VA 23467
www.joyministriesonline.org

ISBN: 978-1-60374-184-2
Printed in the United States of America
© 2010 by Danette Joy Crawford

Whitaker House
1030 Hunt Valley Circle
New Kensington, PA 15068
www.whitakerhouse.com

Library of Congress Cataloging-in-Publication Data

Crawford, Danette Joy, 1965–
  Don't quit in the pit / by Danette Joy Crawford.
    p. cm.
  ISBN 978-1-60374-184-2 (trade pbk. : alk. paper) 1. Suffering—Religious aspects—
Christianity. 2. Success—Religious aspects—Christianity. I. Title.
  BV4909.C73 2010
  248.8'6—dc22
                            2009038727

1 2 3 4 5 6 7 8 9 10 11 **LU** 17 16 15 14 13 12 11 10

Dedication

This book is dedicated to my mother, Deborah. Thank you for always believing in me and for being a great source of unconditional love and encouragement!

Acknowledgments

First and foremost, I want to thank the Lord for His unfailing, unconditional love for me. Without God, I would have quit in the pit a long time ago. Thank You, Lord, for saving my soul and filling me with Your precious Holy Spirit.

To my daughter, Destiny—thank you for filling my life with joy and laughter, and thank you for your patience and understanding during the many months that I have spent writing this book. I am so proud of you and your heart for God, and I know He is going to do great things through your life.

To my family and friends—thank you for believing in me and encouraging me along the way, and for your help during the writing process of this book.

To my spiritual mentors—thank you for being godly examples and leading the way for me to come into my full potential.

To the most awesome staff and intercessors anyone could ever have—the Joy Ministries Team. Thank you for standing with me through prayer, long hours of work, and your mountain-moving faith. Thank you for your passion for the Lord, your desire to see souls saved, and your heart to see lives changed. We truly are a team, and without you, Joy Ministries would not be what it is today.

To my most precious partners—without your giving of time, prayer, and financial support, Joy Ministries could not do everything it is doing today. Thank you! Together, we are transforming lives, healing hearts, and saving souls.

Finally, to Bob Whitaker and the entire staff at Whitaker House—thank you for your heart to minister to people through the printed word. Thank you for believing in me and for being such a great team to work with. It has been an honor to work with you.

Foreword

All of us face storms that test our character and our faith. Danette Joy Crawford's book *Don't Quit in the Pit* is an inspiring story of the faithfulness of God. Filled with hope, encouragement, and healing to those with broken lives and shattered dreams, her book provides important keys to successfully getting to the other side of whatever storm you may be facing in your life.

Danette Joy Crawford is a bold woman of faith who will inspire you to keep the fire for Jesus burning strong. She reaches out to people to meet not only their spiritual needs, but also their physical and emotional needs. She can bring hope to others because she has experienced being in the pit and has learned how not to stay there. The pit is only temporary—so, don't quit in the pit. Danette's story will inspire you, build your faith, and bring you to a new level of trust in God! I highly recommend *Don't Quit in the Pit* to *every* Christian.

—*Marilyn Hickey*
Founder and President, Marilyn Hickey Ministries
Author, *The Names of God*

Contents

Introduction

On any given day, we find ourselves on a peak, in a pit, or somewhere in between. We'd love to remain on the peaks of life—those times of extreme joy and gladness. Unfortunately, though, a lot of people spend too much of their time in a pit, whether it's a pit of emotional despair, financial hardship, mental anguish, physical pain, or something else. What's even more unfortunate is that many people park in the pit and never get out. Discouraged and defeated, they decide to remain where they are instead of determining to escape their pit and climb the next peak. Don't allow this to be your fate! You can't afford to park in the pit. Your life—and your ultimate destiny—depend on your determining to trust God and get out.

Don't Park in the Pit

In my years of ministry, I have met many people who have been in the midst of seemingly hopeless situations. Tragically, I have seen people park in their pits, never to escape. But I have had the sheer joy of seeing others decide to get out of the pit and overcome difficult circumstances. Dee[*] is just one of them.

Dee felt trapped. For generations, her family had lived in subsidized housing, and it looked doubtful that she'd break the trend. The single mother of three lived with the father of her children—and suffered his emotional, mental, and verbal abuse day after day. Dee lived her life in a pit of pain and lack, with no escape in sight. All that began to change, however, due to a seemingly simple decision that would turn her life around.

[*] *Name has been changed to protect identity.*

We were holding an outreach in Dee's housing development, and Dee came out of her home to a temporary meeting area we had set up to receive one of the bags of groceries we were giving away. In addition to the groceries, she received something far more important: salvation. She gave her life to the Lord during the altar call, a decision that started her climb out of the pit. The following day, my daughter and I knocked on her door to give her a Bible and invite her to church. Immediately, Dee joined our ministry's Single Moms' LIFE Group, where she developed relationships with supportive Christian women. She brought her children to our weekly kids club, where they, too, gave their lives to the Lord. Later, she enrolled them in our summer reading camp, where they learned to read. As Dee became more involved in our outreaches and matured in her faith, she made the decision to get out of her abusive relationship.

And she didn't stop there. She made another decision to get a job and, with the assistance of our Back to Work program, found employment and got off welfare. With the help of our ministry, she moved out of subsidized housing and into her own home. Determined to get an education, Dee enrolled at a college and earned a degree in medical assisting. Today, more than ten years after her life-altering decision, Dee has a great career, and she and her children love the Lord. What an amazing turnaround!

Are you looking up from a dark pit with high walls and no ladder in sight, like Dee had been? If so, I want to extend a rope of hope to you! Your situation may seem hopeless. Your pain may be overwhelming. Yet there is Someone who knows your sorrows even better than you do, and He will bring you out of your pit, just as He did for Dee. Even in your pit, you're not alone; the Lord is with you, no matter how deep and dark your pit may be.

> **THE LORD IS WITH YOU, NO MATTER HOW DEEP AND DARK YOUR PIT MAY BE.**

God's Proven Track Record of Rescues from the Pit

If you feel like you're in a pit, relax. You're not the first person to find yourself looking up from within what feels like a deep, dark hole. In the Old Testament of the Bible, we read about a guy named Joseph who found himself in his own pit—literally! For Joseph, that pit looked like a dark dead end, but it was truly a pathway to the palace—a direct route, at that. (See Genesis 37:5–36; 39; 41:14–44.)

In the New Testament, we read about the apostle Paul, a respected Jewish leader who became a Christian, won souls for Jesus, and consequently found himself in his own pit. Paul's pit was in the form of a ship tossed in a raging storm. Everybody wanted to jump off the boat, but God told Paul, "Don't abandon ship—you'll come through this!" (See Acts 27.)

You see, being in a pit is a situation common to all people—male and female, rich and poor, young and old. I want to encourage you today— don't abandon ship! Yes, your pit may seem overwhelming. Yes, you may be in the midst of the biggest storm of your life. But I can promise you that it's temporary. When you trust your Father God and obey Him, He will guide you out of the pit. This, too, shall pass.

Grab Hold of the Word—Your Rope of Hope

Both Joseph and Paul needed a rope of hope to climb out of the pit. Their rope of hope was the same one that's available for you—God's Word. The Bible provides a map to guide us out of any and every pit that we find ourselves in. Psalm 34:19 says, *"Many are the afflictions of the righteous, but the LORD delivers him out of them all"* (NKJV). In other words, we all will experience "pits" in our lives—they're inevitable—but we can escape when we grab hold of the rope of hope and determine to climb out.

Read It, 'Cause You'll Need It!

I travel a lot by car, but I don't like to use a GPS. So, I always study a map before I leave to go somewhere. If I don't study the map beforehand or refer to it during my trip, I'm almost guaranteed to get lost. Arriving at my planned destination is as easy as reading the map, but I have to *read* it—I can't automatically absorb knowledge of the route. And the same rule is true regarding our map out of the pit. We have to *read* the Word of truth— the Bible, which is our map! John 8:32 says, *"You will know the truth, and the truth will set you free."* The truth on its own doesn't set you free; it's the truth that you *know* that sets you free.

The good news is that every pit has the potential to be temporary because the Word promises that God will deliver us from every affliction. The rope of hope—God's Word—will never disappoint us. *"Then you will know that I am the LORD; those who hope in me will not be disappointed"* (Isaiah 49:23). Isn't that a precious promise? We have a Friend, our wonderful Father, who never lets us down. When our hope is in Him, we are never disappointed. When our hope is in another person, a paycheck, or a situation, the day will come when we are disappointed. But when our hope is in the Lord, we will never be disappointed.

I think of the Bible story of Abraham and Sarah. This couple had waited years and years to have a baby. Abraham knew that his body was now too old, and he'd never met one woman who had conceived a child at Sarah's age. Besides, even when Sarah had been younger, she'd been barren.

But Abraham didn't hold on to the facts in front of him. He held on to a rope of hope that God had thrown him, and, at one hundred years of age, he was still hanging on!

> *Against all hope, Abraham in hope believed and so became the father of many nations, just as it had been said to him, "So shall your offspring be." Without weakening in his faith, he faced the fact that his body was as good as dead—since he was about a hundred years old—and that Sarah's womb was also dead. Yet he did not waver through unbelief regarding the promise of God, but was strengthened in his faith and gave glory to God, being fully persuaded that God had power to do what he had promised.* (Romans 4:18–21)

Wow! Against all hope in the natural realm, Abraham clung to the rope of hope by believing the Word of God. God had given him a promise, and he believed it! He didn't deny the facts; he faced them and dealt with them in a powerful, fruitful way. The facts exist in the natural realm, but the truth—God's Word—exists in the spirit realm. The truth always outweighs the facts. And when we place our hope in the truth, as Abraham did, our faith can change the facts!

I am living proof of this truth, but it was a hard lesson to learn—one that brought me through many personal "pit stops." Or, maybe I should say "pit pauses," because I had to be determined not to remain stuck in the pits.

My prayer is that this book will encourage you to make your times in the pit temporary seasons. Maybe you are in a financial pit, an emotional pit, a health pit, a relational pit, or even a spiritual pit today. I want you to be determined never to quit in the pit, but always to grab hold of the rope of hope—God's Word—and make your way to the palace.

—1—

A Personal Pit

I grew up on a farm in Maryland, where my brothers and I regularly helped out with chores. My father worked hard, and to this day, I believe that my strong work ethic and keen wisdom in finances come from him. Today, some people would probably call my father a workaholic: when he wasn't doing work for the family business of well-water drilling, he was working on the farm, and about the only time he spent with his children was when we were helping him. We baled hay, fed cows, and did other farm chores.

After we'd worked in the fields all day, our reward was working the crank on the ice cream maker. Our extended family members, along with friends and neighbors, would gather in the evenings at our little home in the country. They always managed to schedule their arrival just right—late enough to avoid working in the fields, but early enough to join us for ice cream!

Those family members and friends, who served vital roles in our lives, did not know about the turmoil that was beginning to stir within our home. Although they were right around us, it took them years to find out about what had been happening behind closed doors. From the outside, our redbrick farmhouse on the hill appeared to be a dream home—but on the inside, we were a family in chaos. Physical and verbal abuse became a frequent occurrence and filled the air in my home, and, at an early age, I started to master the art of suppressing feelings, emotional wounds, and, perhaps most devastating, a strong sense of rejection.

A Badge of Shame

One day, I was about to enter the kitchen when I stopped in the doorway and cringed. My parents were having another argument, and this one was getting violent. The yelling and screaming somehow didn't match the cheery, red-checkered tablecloth and plaid vinyl chairs at the kitchen table.

Suddenly, Dad picked up my Girl Scout Brownie Bank.

No! I screamed inside. But nothing came out of my mouth.

Thud.

He hit Mom in the head with the bank, and the uproar of the argument was replaced with a terrifying silence. The woman who was my only sense of stability lay there so still, so quiet. Quite frightened, I wondered, *Is she dead?*

"Mom! Mom! Are you okay? Are you all right?" I ran over to her, dropped to my knees, and yelled over and over again, hysterical and trembling, with tears running down my face. "Mom!"

This went on for some time until she finally stirred, and I helped her get up. Dad was gone—relief swept over me. But my Brownie Bank was in a million pieces. As I gathered the remains of our troop's prized possession, I hung my head in shame and wept. *How will I explain this to the girls in the Brownie troop?* I wondered.

Part of my daily existence in a dysfunctional home was covering up the signs that my life was upside-down. The sense of shame about what was going on at home was horrible, and I felt that I had to hide it. I felt guilty for lying, but, even more, I felt ashamed, so I made excuses to conceal what had happened to the treasured Brownie Bank.

I wore shame like a badge—the shame of covering up for my dad. I was embarrassed because everyone around me seemed to have an ideal family unit, while I didn't.

Adults would ask me, "Where is your dad?"

One day, a friend commented, "I never see your dad at your house."

Her words rushed over me and pushed me into a corner. I valued this girl's opinion of me, and her words made me panic. I thought, *What if she finds out?* I felt that lying was the only way out.

"Oh, he's a truck driver," I answered. "He's never home because he's a truck driver."

I habitually lied and made up excuses because he wasn't there.

Eating in Fear

I'm not sure when it began, but at some point along the way, I picked up a number of nervous habits—compulsive quirks that were essentially attempts to stuff down the wounds and fears that I experienced inside my farmhouse on the hill.

One evening, the five of us were sitting around the kitchen table with the red-checkered tablecloth, our plates filled with steaming food. As usual, I was required to eat every bite. My stomach churned; I didn't want to anger my father, who was sitting across from me. Nervous, I blinked my eyes profusely, and he told me to stop it. Fear tingled down my spine.

I can't stop! I thought.

In an attempt to control my blinking, I stretched my mouth once, then stretched it again, pulling my lips, perhaps willing them to widen enough to inhale all of the food in front of me. Most of the time when I did this, Dad ignored me. But I could tell that this night would be different.

"Stop doing that!" he demanded.

I did it again. I couldn't stop. I blinked and stretched my mouth, trying to hold back the tears, grasping for some mechanism that would help me stop my nervous habits.

"STOP!"

My father reached out and grabbed the yardstick.

Whack.

My face stung. Tears fell.

"Eat all your food—now."

I continued crying as I choked down my food as best I could, then asked to be dismissed from the dinner table. In just one meal, my sense of self-worth had fallen as fast as my tears, and my self-esteem had plummeted.

As the shame and pain increased with each incident, so did my nervous habits and my attempts to suppress the emotional wounds and the overwhelming sense of rejection. Yet many years would pass before I would understand that my attempts to deal on my own with everything going on around me were not completely successful. The practice of suppressing my feelings was devastating to my emotions. I suppressed things for so long, I became numb—which was actually the desired result, even though it wasn't healthy.

People would ask me if my dad was an alcoholic. But my dad didn't drink—he worked. And after my little brother was born, he was gone more than ever before. He started going out at night with his friends, and then, as I found out later, he began meeting various women. At the time, I knew only that my dad was absent from our home and was disconnected and disengaged from our family unit. To my mother, his lifestyle was devastating.

As I said before, there were many fights at home. My parents' anger and rage would come out both verbally and physically, often with objects thrown through the air, and, like many children whose parents fight constantly or get divorced, I blamed myself.

Mom and I were alone in the house the day she overdosed on pills. Today, I realize that she felt hopeless, and her suicide attempt was an outward symptom of a deep, internal cry for help. I don't believe she really wanted to die; she just couldn't live the way she was living anymore.

I found out about her overdose because I was right there when she picked up the phone and called Dr. Meadows, a man she'd once worked for. He treated her like one of his own daughters, and she knew that he cared about her.

"I've taken an overdose," she told him. "I'm going to die."

I stayed at Mom's side. Dr. Meadows must have called for an ambulance, for suddenly, sirens surrounded our country house, and medics came into our kitchen, questioning my mom. When they left to take her to the hospital, I wanted to go with them, but they wouldn't let me.

So much of this incident is a blur to me now—a blur of pain that I tried to stuff down for years. What I remember most now is the loneliness and fear I felt when the ambulance left me standing there in my neighbors' yard across the street, watching the ambulance take my mom away and wondering if she'd ever come back. I was an emotional wreck.

A Child's Spiritual Hunger

When I was a child, I couldn't go to sleep at night unless I'd prayed first. I didn't know about being born again, but I always prayed.

As a young child, I had a passion for attending church. Ironically, we lived on Brown Church Road! On Sundays, my parents would drop me off at a little country church with stained-glass windows.

However, as I grew older, and the difficulties and drama in my home escalated, I began to feel as though I was inferior to the other kids at church. Children get a sense of security and self-worth when there is stability at home; my sense of security and my self-worth were plummeting at this point. Little by little, my passion for church attendance waned because, as I looked around me at all the other kids my age, I saw myself in comparison and came to the following conclusions:

+ *They have more money.*
+ *Their parents are together.*
+ *They have perfect little families.*
+ *I don't feel connected.*
+ *I don't fit in.*

Finally, after my parents divorced and we moved to another town, I decided I didn't want to go to Sunday school anymore. I had that attitude until I got saved at the age of seventeen.

Suicidal Thoughts

The hurts and wounds that I had tried to suppress had begun to surface during my early teenage years. I began to get depressed and even contemplated suicide myself. One night, when I was on the verge of a total breakdown, my mom took me to the emergency room at the local hospital, where they recommended I receive outpatient counseling with a psychiatrist. Oddly enough, they referred me to the same psychiatrist who had worked with my mom when she'd been hospitalized years earlier. I realized that God had sent this doctor into my life because I'd been ready to end it all.

To this day, I know that God had His hand on me, gently leading and guiding me to His plan for my life. He was preparing me to meet the great I Am, and I was about to change counselors! Although this secular psychiatrist gave me some ungodly advice, God was overseeing the big picture. He was working in my heart to prepare me for what was to come—to receive Him as Lord and Savior.

> TO THIS DAY, I KNOW THAT GOD HAD HIS HAND ON ME, GENTLY LEADING AND GUIDING ME TO HIS PLAN FOR MY LIFE.

An Unlikely Invitation to Church

My grandparents lived near us, as well as near a little country church, and from their house, we could hear the music coming from the church during its services. We would get together at Grandma's and laugh at the "Holy Rollers" who attended the church and make comments, such as "Boy, those Holy Rollers were really rolling last night!" I can remember picturing what I thought was happening inside at the services.

When I was seventeen, out of the blue, my dad asked if he could take me somewhere. It was hard for me to believe he was asking me to come with him, and it was even harder for me to believe where he wanted to take me—to that Holy Roller church! I quickly responded, "I don't think so!"

I found out that Dad had started dating a woman who attended that church, and she'd been a positive influence in his life. He, in turn, wanted to have a positive impact on me by taking me to church.

I successfully dodged his invitation for months. But one night in late summer, my luck ran out—or did it? I was sitting at home with nothing to do when my dad paid me an unexpected and unforgettable visit. I couldn't use my normal excuse because I didn't have any plans with my friends or boyfriend, so I reluctantly gave in to his request to attend a church service. It was a Sunday evening, and my first thought was, *I can't believe these people go to church on both Sunday morning and Sunday night!* When I asked my dad about this, he told me that some weeks, he even went to church on Thursday nights, too! I thought to myself, *Well, that's just another confirmation to me that these "Jesus Freaks" really are crazy!*

The previous summer, my former boyfriend had returned from a summer trip to Texas to inform me that he had been born again. I'd dumped him immediately because I hadn't wanted anything to do with those Jesus Freaks.

Now, here I was, about to do what I'd said I would never do. As soon as I entered that little country church at the bottom of Brown Church Road, my thoughts were validated. These folks were definitely different! They kept shouting "Hallelujah!" and "Praise the Lord!" They were singing, all right, as well as clapping their hands or raising them in the air and mumbling weird-sounding words. I decided to sit in the back. *This way,* I thought, *I can sneak out as soon as the service ends—just in case the Holy Rollers roll really late tonight!*

Everyone except me had his or her eyes closed. I was actually in a state of shock. First and foremost, I couldn't believe that I was actually there; second, I kept waiting for them to roll around on the floor. After all, that was why everyone called them "Holy Rollers," right?

I was surprised when no one rolled on the floor, and I was even more surprised when the pastor started preaching. Not only was his message interesting, but it was also as if he was preaching directly to me. I began to look around the room to see if there was anybody there whom I knew, thinking, *Surely, someone must have told him about my life and let him know that I was coming tonight.* I saw a young girl named Hope who lived in my neighborhood and immediately concluded that she must have told Pastor White all about me. Later, though, I realized that I had never told Hope about any of that stuff.

As the service came to a close, the pastor asked for all those who wanted to accept Jesus into their hearts as their Lord and Savior to come to the front of the church. I immediately thought, *That's what the difference is—I need what he's talking about. That's me!* But the thought of going forward in front of what seemed to be a massive crowd was overwhelming to me. All of my insecurities, all of my inferiorities, and all of my fears had reached a level that made me feel inhibited in front of people, especially people I didn't know.

Coming to Salvation over the Phone

As much as I wanted to respond to the tugging in my heart, I was held back by my emotional baggage. Yet I quickly came up with a plan, and, when Dad dropped me off at my house, I thanked him for inviting me before running excitedly to my room to call Hope. Over the phone, I asked her if she had ever told Pastor White anything about me or my life. I was amazed to find out that she had not. She explained to me that the Holy Spirit knew everything about me, and that it had been He who had instructed Pastor White. I opened up and told Hope about the desire I'd had to go forward at the service, and she informed me that I could pray and ask Jesus into my heart on the telephone with her.

"On the telephone?" I questioned. "Don't you have to be at a church to do that?"

Just moments later, God used this young girl to lead me in a prayer that would change my life forever. Looking back, I'm in awe that God would use my dad and a girl named Hope to bring such desperately needed *hope* into my life.

After praying, I told her, "I don't feel any different. Maybe I have just done too many bad things for God to really forgive me."

Hope instructed me to ask the Lord to show me that He was real in my life, and that He had, indeed, forgiven me. Before I went to sleep that night, I prayed and asked the Lord those very things. I had been having trouble sleeping for many months, but that night, I quickly drifted off into a deep, peaceful sleep. Sometime in the early-morning hours, for no apparent reason, my eyes opened. Lying in bed, I noticed that my desk lamp was on. Puzzled, I pulled back the covers and went to turn it off. As my feet hit the floor, it felt as though I was walking on clouds. I proceeded to my desk and gently turned the knob to the off position.

As I walked back to my bed, I again felt as though clouds were beneath my feet. When my head hit the pillow, the Lord said with such clarity, "I'm the light of your life. From this day forward, follow Me."

> GOD HAD HEARD MY PRAYER, AND HE'D ANSWERED ME IMMEDIATELY. HE REALLY HAD FORGIVEN ME. HE REALLY HAD SAVED ME.

Wow! God had heard my prayer, and He'd answered me immediately. He really had forgiven me. He really had saved me. He really had spoken to me. I drifted off into a deep sleep, the best night's sleep that I could remember having. The next morning, I asked my mom if she had turned on my lamp in the middle of the night. After she responded, "No," I explained everything to her and began to rejoice in the new peace and joy that I had found.

By this time, I had been in counseling for one year. At my next session, I announced to my psychiatrist that I had been saved. It was a short while later that I realized I had found the answer to my many needs in my new relationship with the Lord. I, too, was now officially one of those Jesus Freaks who attended the Holy Roller church, and I couldn't be happier!

Is God Calling You, Too?

Maybe, today, you feel like I did years ago. Have you experienced so much emotional brokenness that you don't exactly know which end is up? Maybe you have thought about God but have never taken that step to accept Him into your life as your personal Savior. As a child, I prayed every night, but I didn't pray a prayer of salvation and accept Christ as my Savior until I was seventeen years old.

I can tell you confidently that it was Jesus Christ alone who got me out of my pit—a pit of sin and emotional brokenness. The Bible tells us that we have *all* sinned and fall short of God's glory. (See Romans 3:23.) Yet, God loved us so much that He gave His only Son, Jesus, to die on the cross for us, so that we could be forgiven of our sins. *"For God so loved the world that he gave his one and only Son, that whoever believes in him shall not perish but have eternal life"* (John 3:16).

For us to accept this awesome gift of salvation, we simply have to follow the steps outlined for us in Romans 10:9–10:

If you confess with your mouth, "Jesus is Lord," and believe in your heart that God raised him from the dead, you will be saved. For it is with your heart that you believe and are justified, and it is with your mouth that you confess and are saved.

1. We must confess with our mouths that we are sinners and that Jesus is Lord.

2. We must believe in our hearts that Jesus is the Son of God, and that God raised Him from the dead.

I want to invite you to accept Christ into your life as your Savior by saying this simple prayer:

Dear Jesus, I believe that You are the Son of God, and that You died on the cross for me and rose again so that I can be forgiven of my sins. I confess to You this day that I am a sinner. Please forgive me of my sins and come into my heart right now as my Lord and Savior. Amen.

If you prayed that prayer, I want to congratulate you for making the most important decision you will ever make—and for grabbing the strongest rope of hope available to get you out of the pit! I also want to welcome you to the family of God. Make sure you tell as many people as you can that you are now a Christian!

Chapter One: A Personal Pit

Points to Ponder

1. We all have personal stories of the pits we've been in. The storms of life come to us all. Psalm 34:19 says that we will have many afflictions (things that cause us pain, suffering, and distress), but that the Lord will deliver us from them all. Think about the afflictions you've experienced in life. List a few of them in the space below, then reflect on and write about how the Lord delivered you out of them.

2. Think about a difficult situation in your past to which you might have reacted differently, had you known then what you know today about the hope you have in Jesus Christ.

3. If you have already accepted Jesus Christ as your Lord and Savior, what do you remember most about your salvation experience?

4. If you have never accepted Jesus Christ into your heart as your Lord and Savior, you can do so today. Just pray the prayer that is printed at the end of Chapter 1. Be sure to share your happy news with as many people as you can!

Meditate on these Scriptures, speak them aloud, and commit them to memory.

A righteous man may have many troubles, but the LORD *delivers him from them all.* (Psalm 34:19)

Everyone who calls on the name of the Lord will be saved. (Romans 10:13)

Weeping may endure for a night, but joy comes in the morning. (Psalm 30:5 NKJV)

I will say of the Lord, He is my Refuge and my Fortress, my God; on Him I lean and rely, and in Him I [confidently] trust! (Psalm 91:2 AMP)

—2—

From the Pit of Rejection to the Peak of Acceptance

Unfortunately, the stronghold of rejection that had taken root in my life lasted many years before I was saved and learned who I was in Christ. Growing up, I was unfamiliar with such Scripture passages as Isaiah 41:9, which says, *"I took you from the ends of the earth, from its farthest corners I called you. I said, 'You are my servant'; I have chosen you and have not rejected you."*

The Power of Negative Words

During my childhood, it didn't take long for the feelings of rejection to turn into self-rejection, which became a huge, open door for insecurity. I hated the way I looked, and I became very insecure about most areas of my life. I felt unworthy of looking nice, so I would dress the part. If anyone complimented me, I would feel extremely uncomfortable, and it would make me want to immediately turn the attention away from myself. I was plagued by words that I would hear over and over in my head—words spoken by my father without ill intent and with little thought of the devastating results they would have.

"Look at your teeth! Don't you brush them?"

"Let me see your face. I can't believe how much acne you have!"

To a little girl who was hungry for her father's love, attention, and acceptance, these words rang continually in my ears as another confirmation of my belief: *You are not valued by others; therefore, you are not valuable.*

Many times, words are what put us in a pit—words spoken to us, about us, or even by us. The power of life and death is in our tongues. (See Proverbs 18:21.) When words that don't align with the Word of truth are spoken, we can quickly find ourselves in a pit dug by the power of those words. It is important not to allow anyone to speak negative words over you, and not to speak negative words over yourself.

I know of many people, myself included, who waited years—some, their entire lives—to hear their fathers say, "I am proud of you." Proverbs 15:4 says, *"A gentle tongue [with its healing power] is a tree of life, but willful contrariness…breaks down the spirit"* (AMP).

My father's negative words equaled rejection in my life. When my parents separated, I was glad that their fights had stopped, yet I felt greatly rejected by my father. The root of rejection continued to grow in my life, and the effects became more and more evident.

A Cry for Acceptance

Out of my feelings of rejection came a desperate cry for acceptance, love, and attention, especially from my father. Unaware of my intentions, I set out to make up for my perceived weaknesses or limitations by developing certain positive characteristics to earn my father's love and acceptance. I quickly learned that one way to earn attention from Dad was with my report cards. So, I would work frantically, semester after semester, year after year, to obtain straight As, which I knew would buy me a few minutes of attention and approval from Dad. Although this acceptance might have lasted only five minutes—ten, at the most—it was well worth the effort, in my childish way of thinking.

As I grew up, my cry for acceptance continued as I sought perfection in every area of my life. My brothers and I handled our home situation in our own different ways. I continued on the road of being overly responsible, putting unrealistic expectations on myself in every area of life.

My low self-esteem and thoughts of worthlessness were hidden successfully behind my many accomplishments. I received numerous academic awards, graduated with high honors, worked a job to assist Mom with my growing financial needs as a teenager, and masked the emotional pain quite well. All along, though, I was searching for the love and acceptance that I desperately needed from my father.

Defeating the Stronghold of Rejection

The loss of a parent through divorce or death is just one of many ways by which a spirit of rejection can start to become a stronghold in a life. The spirit of rejection was the greatest stronghold the enemy strategically built in my life as a child. *Strongholds* are arguments and pretensions Satan presents to us that are against the Word of God. Satan pretends they are truth, and he tries to put forth very convincing arguments. However, the Word of God is the ultimate source of truth about everything, including who we are in Christ. And Christ has given us the weapons with which to wage a successful fight against the devil and demolish his every stronghold.

> **THE WORD OF GOD IS THE ULTIMATE SOURCE OF TRUTH ABOUT EVERYTHING, INCLUDING WHO WE ARE IN CHRIST.**

The Word of God, or the *"sword of the Spirit"* (Ephesians 6:17), and the fruit of the Spirit—*"love, joy, peace, patience, kindness, goodness, faithfulness, gentleness and self-control"* (Galatians 5:22–23)—have divine power to demolish Satan's strongholds.

Identify Satan's Lies

For though we live in the world, we do not wage war as the world does. The weapons we fight with are not the weapons of the world. On the contrary, they have divine power to demolish strongholds. We demolish arguments and every pretension that sets itself up against the knowledge of God, and we take captive every thought to make it obedient to Christ. (2 Corinthians 10:3–5)

The devil is such a liar. He tried to snuff out the call of God on my life from the very beginning. He tried, but it isn't over until you and God win! God wins in us and through us when we know who we are in Christ. Our circumstances don't define who we are. Situations that surround us don't define who we are. Other people's words, actions, and thoughts don't define who we are. Only God and His Word define who we are.

I took you from the ends of the earth, from its farthest corners I called you. I said, "You are my servant"; I have chosen you and have not rejected you. So do not fear, for I am with you; do not be dismayed, for I am your God. I will strengthen you and help you; I will uphold you with my righteous right hand. (Isaiah 41:9–10)

That passage is so powerful and encouraging. Our heavenly Father has chosen us and not rejected us. If others reject us, it doesn't even matter, because Father has not rejected us. He has chosen us.

When the devil was establishing a stronghold of rejection in my young life, I lived in that pit of rejection. It was not until a few years after I gave my life to the Lord that I began to practice saying out loud, "I'm not rejected—I'm accepted! I am accepted by Christ." As we speak the Word of truth, we renew our minds. Out with the old lies and in with the truth!

Become Rejection Proof

The devil wants us to be susceptible to rejection, but the Lord wants us to be rejection proof. Society often rejects us if we don't look a certain way, act a certain way, or have a certain income. Society tries to teach our children at an early age to reject those who don't wear brand-name clothes or who talk differently than everyone else. As we live a Christian life in these last days before the second coming of Christ, we need to be rejection proof more than ever so that we can walk boldly with the Lord before an increasingly godless society.

When you know who you are in Christ, receive the unconditional love God has for you, and acknowledge God's acceptance, you'll become what I call "rejection proof." You have to know it in your heart and in your spirit—not just in your mind as head knowledge. And this knowledge comes only when you regularly study and meditate on God's Word and spend time in His presence through prayer and worship.

Proof means "able to resist or repel." Something that is waterproof cannot be penetrated by water. When God and His Word make us rejection proof, rejection cannot penetrate our hearts or our spirits; we are not permanently affected or influenced by rejection, whether it's real or perceived. When we are rejection proof, we are protected from and resistant to other people's negative thoughts, words, and actions.

Resist Perceived Rejection

There are two types of rejection: actual rejection and perceived rejection. Both hurt very badly if we aren't rejection proof. Perceived rejection is a device of the devil, whom the Bible calls the father of lies: *"He [the devil] was a murderer from the beginning, not holding to the truth, for there is no truth in him. When he lies, he speaks his native language, for he is a liar and the father of lies"* (John 8:44). The devil loves it when we feel rejected, and if he can't cause actual rejection to come our way, he'll attempt to mess with our perceptions. I call it "perception deception." Through perception deception, he'll deceive us into thinking that other people are rejecting us.

If, for example, you walk into a room and no one greets you, so people appear to be ignoring you, or everyone suddenly stops talking and it seems like they were talking about you, the devil is trying to make you perceive rejection. He has a heyday trying to get you to feel rejected, and he will wage wars in your mind with thoughts that come straight from the pit of hell.

There is a lady on the staff of my ministry who previously had a root of rejection in her life. Whenever she was corrected, she would interpret it as rejection. I had to explain to her that correction is not the same thing as rejection.

I sensed that the root of rejection in her life had started in her childhood. Sure enough, when she was thirteen, her mother became very sick; she died three years later. After her death, this young woman's father tried desperately to deal with his own pain. Just a few months after his wife's passing, when his children still needed the strong, loving support of their father, he left to stay with a new girlfriend for two months. Eventually, he moved his girlfriend into his home, then married her on the one-year anniversary of his wife's death. His daughter felt a double sting of rejection, for she experienced rejection on her mother's behalf, as well, and went on to interpret many routine events and interactions as further personal rejection.

For example, if we held an office meeting and she wasn't invited, she would feel rejected. While other members of our staff would feel relieved not to be required to attend another meeting, this woman would take it as intentional exclusion. And even when she'd been invited to participate in a meeting or activity, she would often feel excluded. This woman was truly deceived by her perceptions of the way people saw her and treated her.

Today, as a result of God's grace and love, she has overcome the stronghold of rejection. The recovery process required her willingness to acknowledge her issue and allow the Holy Spirit to change her biased perceptions. Now, she serves as a vital member of my staff, and God is using her to minister to others who are dealing with issues of rejection.

The devil's goal is to get you to perceive rejection that isn't there. Don't fall for it! Don't be susceptible to perception deception, but be rejection proof. Renew your mind to the truth and keep on keeping on!

Conquer Your Fears

Do not fear, for I am with you; do not be dismayed, for I am your God. (Isaiah 41:10)

Unless we have an intimate relationship with Christ, the rejection we experience will produce fear in our lives. When the enemy succeeds at causing us to perceive rejection, we usually feel dismayed, afraid, and discouraged. Fear and discouragement are some of Satan's favorite schemes to use against us.

Second Timothy 1:7 gives us this reassurance: *"God has not given us a spirit of fear, but of power and of love and of a sound mind"* (NKJV). God hasn't given us that spirit of fear; the enemy is the one who has thrown it at us. He's trying to cripple us with the fear of rejection, the fear of failure, the fear of people, and so forth.

We must be controlled by the Holy Spirit and not by other people. The Word tells us that the fear of man—including the fear of man's rejection—will entrap us. *"Fear of man will prove to be a snare, but whoever trusts in the LORD is kept safe"* (Proverbs 29:25). And the fear of man is not pleasing to the Lord.

God has given us power and authority in the name of Jesus. Don't throw away your power by

> **FATHER HAS GIVEN YOU THE POWER TO HANDLE AND TO OVERCOME EVERYTHING THAT COMES AGAINST YOU IN THIS LIFE.**

receiving a spirit of fear from the pit of hell! Father has given you the power to handle and to overcome everything that comes against you in this life.

I have given you authority to trample on snakes and scorpions and to overcome all the power of the enemy; nothing will harm you.

(Luke 10:19)

Say, "I am the one with the power!" Never neglect the power the Father has given you by giving in to any spirit of fear, especially the fear of rejection.

Deal with Real Rejection

Although other people may really reject us for various reasons throughout our lives, God never rejects us. Again, He tells us, *"I have chosen you and have not rejected you"* (Isaiah 41:9).

Keeping this in mind, we can have a clear perspective when faced with rejection. If others reject us, we can know that their negative words or actions don't define who we are. Most of the time, those words and actions actually define who *they* are.

Are there any people in your life who continually speak negative things to you and about you? Most likely, their words are actually a reflection of themselves and their misery, hurt, or anger. Maybe they think negatively about themselves, and putting others down makes them feel a little better about themselves. Whatever the case, their words and actions don't define your value or who you are. God's Word defines who you are: His child, fearfully and wonderfully made in His image. (See Psalm 139:14.)

Rejection is a tactic people frequently use to attempt to control and manipulate others' actions, choices, or behavior. Those who reject you may not even be aware that their underlying motive is to control you. Yet only when you do what they want, when and how they want it, do they give you their stamp of approval and withdraw their rejection.

Hurt people hurt other people; as the saying goes, "Misery loves company." People who are miserable often like to make those around them miserable, too. Maybe the people rejecting you have experienced a lot of rejection themselves and have never learned how to relate to other people in healthy ways. As you take a stand and remain rejection proof, the Lord can use you as an example in their lives.

Never play into other people's issues. If they choose to stay stuck there, you can't do anything about it. But you can choose healthy ways of relating to people by not allowing their rejection to control you. Don't let someone else's issue become your issue—you have enough of your own issues to deal with. If others want to reject you, if they want to talk about you, recognize that they have issues and just let them roll off your back. After all, Father has made you rejection proof!

Dealing with Parental Rejection

All too often, people's lives are characterized by a painful lack of significant relationships. The wounds we carry from broken or lost relationships can cripple us emotionally for life if we don't look to the Lord for our healing. Two vital relationships in every person's life are the relationships with Mom and Dad. It is important to have healthy relationships with your mother and father (or a mother and father figure, if a relationship with your biological parents is not possible). Wounds that come from those relationships—or from the utter lack of those relationships—can cause a negative lifestyle directly linked to those wounds.

Broken relationships happen because people, including you and me, are broken. Broken people create broken relationships. You can't give something you don't have. If one or both of your parents never had an example of loving, caring parents, chances are, they don't know how to be loving, caring parents to you.

Examine Your Heart

When we are dealing with the wounds of broken relationships, the first thing the Lord wants us to do is to examine our own hearts. It's easy to point the finger and judge others, but what about us and our hearts? We all must answer to the Lord for what is in our own hearts. Maybe we were rejected or abandoned by one or both of our parents. Maybe we were abused or neglected. No matter what we have been through, we must forgive. We must release anyone who has hurt us, and we must do everything we can to mend every broken relationship. If we have done all that we can do and the wounds are still there, we must turn the relationship over to the Lord. (Actually, it should be surrendered to Him all along.)

Extend Forgiveness

If we don't release those who have hurt and wounded us, we are the ones who suffer the most. It has been medically proven that many health problems, including types of cancer, are often the result of unhealthy emotions, such as anger, hatred, bitterness, unforgiveness, and anxiety. Unhealthy emotions not only cripple us spiritually, but they also can destroy us physically.

Allow the Holy Spirit to search your heart today, and then extend forgiveness to both of your parents, no matter what circumstances you have faced throughout your life. The Word tells us to honor our mothers and fathers. (See, for example, Exodus 20:12.) It doesn't say to honor them if they have done everything right; it says to honor them, regardless of their actions.

The first step in your healing from any wounds stemming from your relationship with your parents is to forgive and honor them. The Word says that if we honor our mothers and fathers, we will have long life. (See Exodus 20:12; Ephesians 6:2–3.) I believe that the opposite is true, as well: we can shorten our lives by harboring ungodly emotions that result in sickness and disease.

Withhold Blame and Judgment

Look to the Lord for the solution to the hurt and pain that you have suffered, and refuse to point the finger in judgment and blame. Maybe you grew up without having a father figure present. Or, maybe your father was physically present but wasn't emotionally available, due to various addictions or his own broken emotions. Maybe you grew up feeling cheated in life because no one was there to cheer you on at your football games or to bring you flowers at your ballet recitals. Maybe you didn't even get to play football or take dance lessons because you had to work to help provide for your family. Whatever your circumstances, the Lord wants you to get past them.

Rejoice in the Faithfulness of Your Heavenly Father

We get past our wounds by focusing on the truth—His Word—which tells us, *"A father to the fatherless, a defender of widows, is God in his holy dwelling"* (Psalm 68:5). God is a Father to the fatherless. Actually, there's a special place in the heart of God for the poor, the fatherless, and the widows. The sooner we understand that He's a Father to the fatherless, the better. But if you are fifty years old and just now finding out, praise God! Growing up, you had a Father that you didn't know about—a heavenly Father. Even though you may have felt all alone at times, you weren't. He loved you then, and He loves you now. You can talk to Him anytime and anywhere in prayer. The Father you always wanted is waiting for you to pour out your heart to Him. And He promises in His Word that He will never leave you nor forsake you.

> *Though my father and mother forsake me, the* Lord *will receive me.*
> (Psalm 27:10)

John 8:32 says, *"You will know the truth, and the truth will set you free."* Now that you know what the Word of Truth says about God's faithfulness and loving acceptance, you can be set free from the bondages and brokenness that a human relationship—or the lack thereof—may have brought into your life.

Helping Your Children Avoid the Pit of Rejection

A child can feel rejection when a parent is present in the room with him but is ignoring him and watching TV instead. We can be physically present in a room and not be emotionally present. As adults, we know it's easy to spend our free time thinking of work we have to do or zoning out in front of the television. But we need to make the effort to give our children attention and even ask them questions so they know that we care about their daily lives. We need to connect emotionally with our kids and really *be* there.

With God's help, we can look at the good and speak the positive over our children. Even when you see negative things, still search for the positive and praise your children for those areas. They need us, their parents, to focus on the good, speak the good, and provide positive reinforcement through words. When correcting our children, we must remember that we need to break their wills but not their spirits. Saying positive words and speaking life over our children can help prevent them from growing up in their own personal pits of rejection.

Chapter Two: From the Pit of Rejection to the Peak of Acceptance

Points to Ponder

1. The devil wants us to be susceptible to rejection, but the Lord wants us to be rejection proof. What does it mean to be *rejection proof*?

   What can you do to become rejection proof?

2. Explain the difference between *perceived* rejection and *real* rejection.

3. What are some ways you have responded to rejection in your life? Were the results hurtful or helpful? Explain how.

4. The rejection we experience may produce fear in our lives. How can we conquer this fear?

5. Why is it important to forgive and release those who have hurt and wounded us?

6. Whom do you need to forgive and release today?

Meditate on these Scriptures, speak them aloud, and commit them to memory.

I took you from the ends of the earth, from its farthest corners I called you. I said, "You are my servant"; I have chosen you and have not rejected you. So do not fear, for I am with you; do not be dismayed, for I am your God. I will strengthen you and help you; I will uphold you with my righteous right hand. (Isaiah 41:9–10)

*Though my father and mother forsake me, the L*ORD *will receive me.* (Psalm 27:10)

*Fear of man will prove to be a snare, but whoever trusts in the L*ORD *is kept safe.* (Proverbs 29:25)

The weapons we fight with are not the weapons of the world. On the contrary, they have divine power to demolish strongholds. (2 Corinthians 10:4)

—3—

From the Pit of Retaliation to the Peak of Restraint

When we experience rejection, our flesh—our sinful nature— often tries to come up with carnal defense mechanisms in order to handle the pain. But this tendency is exactly what Paul said we *shouldn't* have—"*For though we walk in the flesh, we do not war according to the flesh. For the weapons of our warfare are not carnal*" (2 Corinthians 10:3–4 NKJV).

When we face rejection or other painful experiences in our lives, we must run *to* God, not away from Him. You may have experienced rejection from a divorce, from the death of a spouse, or from being married to someone with a sexual addiction. I can honestly say that the worst rejection I ever experienced was being married to a man with a sexual addiction. He was sleeping with everyone in town but me. I kept thinking to myself, *What am I, chopped liver?* Although the pain of rejection is deep, the love of God is deeper.

"*For the* LORD *is good and his love endures forever*" (Psalm 100:5). During times of deep pain, hang on to the love of your heavenly Father. Don't reach for something or someone to numb the pain. That drug, that drink, or that other relationship will only leave you in a greater place of pain. But when you run to your Abba Father (see Romans 8:15), the pain of rejection will decrease, and your sense of His love will escalate.

Don't Repay Sin with Sin

Blessed is the man who perseveres under trial, because when he has stood the test, he will receive the crown of life that God has promised to those who love him. When tempted, no one should say, "God is tempting me." For God cannot be tempted by evil, nor does he tempt anyone; but each one is tempted when, by his own evil desire, he is dragged away and enticed. Then, after desire has conceived, it gives birth to sin; and sin, when it is full-grown, gives birth to death.

(James 1:12–15)

We must never respond to the sins others commit against us by committing sin ourselves. Never allow the enemy to drag you away from God and entice you with sin. Only God and His presence can satisfy. Sin never satisfies. Cut off every ungodly desire before it has a chance to conceive in your life. Don't allow yourself to be around sin or to entertain thoughts of sin. Don't allow yourself to remain in vulnerable situations, but maintain godly boundaries and keep up your guard against the schemes of the enemy. If you allow an ungodly desire to conceive, it will birth sin in your life. If you allow sin to stay in your life, it will become full-grown. Full-grown sin gives birth to death—spiritual death and possibly even physical death.

God loves you, and He wants you to come running into His arms of love today. Bring your pain and place it at His feet. His unconditional love and His presence are all that we need. Nothing truly satisfies but the Lord. The choices of other people can never disqualify us from receiving what God has for us. The only thing that can disqualify us is our choices. If we choose to get up out of our messes and cling to the Lord, everything's going to be all right!

In the parable of the sower, *"Those on the rock are the ones who receive the word with joy when they hear it, but they have no root. They believe for a while, but in the time of testing they fall away"* (Luke 8:13). You need to purpose in your heart never to fall away during times of testing. Emotional pain, especially the pain of rejection, brings great testing. But instead of falling away from the Lord, fall into His loving arms.

Your love, O LORD, reaches to the heavens, your faithfulness to the skies. Your righteousness is like the mighty mountains, your justice like the great deep. O LORD, you preserve both man and beast. How priceless is your unfailing love! (Psalm 36:5–7)

Take a minute right now and lift both hands. Surrender your heart, your pain, and your will to the Lord. He's just waiting for you to call on

His name. As you call on the name of the Lord, He will deliver you and set you free. He's simply waiting on you. Don't delay—call on His name today.

Joseph Experienced the Ultimate Rejection yet Resisted Retaliation

When [Joseph's] brothers saw that their father loved him more than any of them, they hated him and could not speak a kind word to him. Joseph had a dream, and when he told it to his brothers, they hated him all the more. (Genesis 37:4–5)

Joseph is the perfect example of someone who was rejection proof. He did not react to the rejection he experienced by sinning himself. He didn't run away from the Lord; He ran to the Lord. He maintained a pure heart. As a result, the Lord was with him wherever he went, and Joseph was successful in everything he did.

> JOSEPH MAINTAINED A PURE HEART. AS A RESULT, THE LORD WAS WITH HIM WHEREVER HE WENT, AND JOSEPH WAS SUCCESSFUL IN EVERYTHING HE DID.

Joseph Knew His Identity in Christ

Joseph was rejection proof because he knew who he was in God before rejection came his way. God had already revealed to Joseph in a dream what he was going to do. What God had said about him in two revelatory dreams spoke louder than what his brothers would say and do to reject him.

So when Joseph came to his brothers, they stripped him of his robe—the richly ornamented robe he was wearing—and they took him and threw him into the cistern....As they sat down to eat their meal, they looked up and saw a caravan of Ishmaelites coming from Gilead. Their camels were loaded with spices, balm and myrrh, and they were on their way to take them down to Egypt. Judah said to his brothers, "What will we gain if we kill our brother and cover up his blood? Come, let's sell him to the Ishmaelites and not lay our hands on him; after all, he is our brother, our own flesh and blood." His brothers agreed. So when the Midianite merchants came by, his brothers pulled Joseph up out of the

cistern and sold him for twenty shekels of silver to the Ishmaelites, who
took him to Egypt. (Genesis 37:23–24, 25–28)

Joseph's own brothers were the ones rejecting him, which made the
sting of rejection that much stronger—betrayal always hurts the most
when it's committed by those closest to us. If we aren't rejection proof, we
can become bitter and angry and then cease to prosper. But because Joseph
was rejection proof, he continued to prosper and be blessed.

When his master saw that the LORD was with him and that the LORD
gave him success in everything he did, Joseph found favor in his eyes
and became his attendant. Potiphar put him in charge of his household,
and he entrusted to his care everything he owned. (Genesis 39:3–4)

Joseph Kept His Cool

Joseph kept his heart right. He never allowed anger to take root and
become fertile soil for bitterness and unforgiveness. He never even allowed frustration to steal his peace. When we lose our peace, we are pulled
right out of the presence of the Lord. Joseph kept his cool and guarded his
peace. Later, the poor guy was even thrown into prison, although he had
done no wrong. But because he was rejection proof, even in prison, Joseph
prospered.

At God's appointed time, Joseph was remembered in prison, and he
was headed for his destiny. He interpreted Pharaoh's dream and was put in
charge of the wealth of the kingdom of Egypt. Joseph came forth into his
purpose. (See Genesis 41:14–44.) If Joseph had not been rejection proof, he
would not have been where he needed to be in order to fulfill his purpose.
Not only did Joseph forgive his brothers and not blame them for what he
had gone through, but he even encouraged them to forgive *themselves!* (See
Genesis 45:4–5.) Now that's character!

Joseph Expected God to Make a Miracle out of His Mess

Joseph knew that God was in charge, working all things together for
his good. (See Genesis 50:20.) And God will do the same for us if we keep
our hearts right. Maybe God is working on your behalf but you can't see it
right now. Even if the enemy is trying to steal, kill, and destroy in your life,

the promise of God to you is that Father will work all things together for your good—if only you keep your heart right.

Expect God to Bring Blessings Out of Your Pain, Too

It amazes me that God works all things together for our good. Romans 8:28 says, *"And we know that in all things God works for the good of those who love him, who have been called according to his purpose."* In other words, it's a bummer if we didn't have a mother or a father growing up, but God will work *all* things together for our good. You might think, *How can God work any good out of this mess?* Well, He will, if you open your eyes and your heart to Him. Allow God to work compassion in your heart for others going through the same difficulties. Start reaching out to others and allow God to use you to be a blessing to someone else. We must get our eyes off of ourselves and get our hearts on the needs of others around us.

When my mom's mother left her suddenly at a young age, my mother purposed in her heart to be a great mother someday—and I can testify that she is the greatest! To this day, I tell everyone that I have the best mother in the world. We must refuse to sit around feeling sorry for ourselves and instead purpose in our hearts to make a difference in the lives of others.

Persevere in Uprooting a Spirit of Rejection

The longer a stronghold of rejection has been present, the longer it usually takes to uproot it. I say "usually" because I've seen God deliver people instantly. For me, overcoming rejection was a gradual process. As I grew in the knowledge of God's Word and in the knowledge of who I am in Christ, I became freer and freer. The Lord would allow what I call "Holy Ghost setups." He would set me up to go to a new level of being rejection proof. Circumstances would throw rejection my way, and I would have to choose to be rejection proof. Others would reject me and speak negatively about me, and I would stand on the Word, speaking forth what God says about me. Each time, I climbed to a greater level of being rejection proof.

Was it always easy? Definitely not. But it was what I needed in order to be healed and become stronger. If we are ever going to do anything for

GOD WILL USE REJECTION FROM OTHER PEOPLE TO FULFILL HIS PURPOSE IN OUR LIVES.

God, we had better be rejection proof. I have probably received more rejection from Christians than from those in the world. This is similar to what Joseph experienced in being rejected by his own brothers. Just remember, the enemy is not flesh and blood! (See Ephesians 6:12.) And don't forget the words of Joseph: *"You intended to harm me, but God intended it for good"* (Genesis 50:20). God will use rejection from other people to fulfill His purpose in our lives.

Don't Build Walls of Isolation

One of my most common defense mechanisms when facing rejection was to put up a wall around myself so that no one could ever hurt me again. The biggest problem with putting up walls is that no one can get in—including those who really love us and care about us, those with whom we need to be in relationship. Yes, our walls may temporarily prevent us from getting hurt, but they also isolate us. It's lonely behind those walls. No love can get in, and no love can get out—including the healthy kind.

Walls will never make us rejection proof; they will only make us lonely and set us up to fall for unhealthy relationships. Our walls will last only so long before they come crashing down. And when they do come crashing down, we may be left vulnerable to involvement in unhealthy relationships, all because we have been isolated.

The Lord is the only One who can make us rejection proof. During the process, He will teach us how to build healthy boundaries—but not walls. We need to have healthy boundaries, and we need to keep our guards up; however, we're not to live in isolation behind self-erected walls.

First Corinthians 16:13 tells us, *"Be on your guard; stand firm in the faith; be men [and women] of courage; be strong."* We must be on guard, for our enemy *"prowls around like a roaring lion looking for someone to devour"* (1 Peter 5:8). We must stay on guard in prayer and keep up our defenses by being aware of the enemy's schemes, but we must take our walls down.

Building emotional walls is a type of carnal attempt to keep ourselves from getting hurt again. I can't promise that you will never get hurt again.

After all, Jesus was despised and rejected by people (see Isaiah 53:3), and we, His people, will be rejected sometimes, as well. Jesus told His disciples,

> *If the world hates you, keep in mind that it hated me first. If you belonged to the world, it would love you as its own. As it is, you do not belong to the world, but I have chosen you out of the world. That is why the world hates you. Remember the words I spoke to you: "No servant is greater than his master." If they persecuted me, they will persecute you also.* (John 15:18–20)

Although I can't promise you'll never get hurt again, I can promise you that building "walls" is not the way to go. God used several special friends at different times in my life to "love my walls down." These special women of God are still in my life today.

The Lord is saying to you, "No more walls!" Stop trying to control all of your relationships out of the fear of rejection, conflict, and emotional wounds. Let the love of God tear those walls down. There are people who love you and care about you. Let the Lord love you through those special people who are already in your life and those whom He wants to bring into your life.

Overcoming Anger

One day, when I was in my early twenties, the Lord spoke to me and said, "You are angry at the world." I was shocked by what He said, yet I immediately began to think about it. Have you ever noticed that God will say things to you that you would never hear from anyone else? If someone else had told me that, I would have gotten defensive. But with God, you don't really have an argument—if you're smart, that is!

As I pondered what He had revealed to me, the truth began to unfold in greater detail. He showed me that a root of anger was affecting my life, and that the anger was my response to the rejection I had perceived as coming from my father. Whenever we feel rejected or unvalued, it's normal to feel angry. Anger is a God-given emotion that rises up within us when we have been mistreated, when we see others being mistreated, or when we encounter other forms of injustice. The Bible tells us, *"Be angry, and do not sin"* (Ephesians 4:26 NKJV). From this verse, we know that it isn't wrong to be angry, but it is wrong to sin within the context of anger.

Be Slow to Become Angry

> *My dear brothers, take note of this: Everyone should be quick to listen, slow to speak and slow to become angry, for man's anger does not bring about the righteous life that God desires.* (James 1:19–20)

> *It is to a man's honor to avoid strife, but every fool is quick to quarrel.* (Proverbs 20:3)

> *An angry man stirs up dissension, and a hot-tempered one commits many sins.* (Proverbs 29:22)

> *Do not repay evil with evil or insult with insult, but with blessing, because to this you were called so that you may inherit a blessing.* (1 Peter 3:9)

Although we can be angry and not sin, the Word tells us numerous times to be slow to become angry. The Lord is slow to become angry, and He abounds in love. *"The LORD is gracious and compassionate, slow to anger and rich in love"* (Psalm 145:8).

We should be the same way. Most of the time, though, we are the opposite—quick to anger and slow to love. We don't want to get these two backward. When we become angry, it doesn't bring about the righteous life that God desires for us to live.

When we have a root of anger in our lives, we are quick to become angry and find it easy to fly off the handle at every little thing that annoys us. A root of anger will cause us to live in constant frustration and inner turmoil; we will erupt like volcanoes, spew out angry words, and exhibit other destructive behaviors.

None of this brings about the righteousness of Christ in our lives. We must choose to allow the Holy Spirit to dig out the root cause of our anger and take it to the cross. As we lay our brokenness before the Lord, the Holy Spirit will heal us and set us free. All we need to do is cry out to the Lord and choose to release those who have hurt and wounded us by forgiving them.

Withhold Blame

The nature of our flesh is to blame someone else when we experience pain or other undesirable circumstances. If you suddenly stub your toe while walking around the house, it's likely that you'll immediately yell and want to blame whoever is nearby. One time, I was sitting in a new car when I dumped a forty-two-ounce drink all over the floor. I immediately started yelling at the person sitting beside me. Of course, it wasn't her fault, but the flesh immediately looks for someone else to blame. As far as the flesh goes, things haven't changed that much since the garden of Eden, where Adam blamed Eve, and Eve blamed the serpent. Sound familiar?

When faced with the unpleasant feeling of rejection, therefore, the first response of our flesh is usually anger. Most of the time, that anger is directed at the person whom we perceive is rejecting us. Psalm 4:4–5 says, *"In your anger do not sin; when you are on your beds, search your hearts and be silent. Offer right sacrifices and trust in the Lord."* In other words, we are not to sin out of anger, nor are we to look for someone else to be the scapegoat for the troubles that we face. Instead, we are to search our own hearts and put our trust in the Lord.

Don't Stay Angry

We must heed the apostle Paul's instructions in Ephesians 4:26–27: *"'In your anger do not sin': Do not let the sun go down while you are still angry, and do not give the devil a foothold."* He was saying, in effect, that it's all right to get angry—but it's not all right to stay angry. By the end of the day—by sundown—make sure you have released the person who has angered you by forgiving him or her. Sometimes, you may have to stay up and have a late-night prayer meeting, but don't allow the anger to remain with you. Any anger that is allowed to stay in our hearts can give the devil a foothold in our lives. No matter what someone has done to hurt you, it's never worth it to hang on to your anger, and it's never pleasing to the Lord.

Every night, we should ask the Holy Spirit to search our hearts as we fulfill the command of Psalm 4:4. If we allow Him to, the Holy Spirit will show us any offenses we have picked up and any wrong heart attitudes we have exhibited throughout the day. After we ask the Holy Spirit to reveal these things to us, we need to be silent before the Lord and wait for Him to speak to us. Too often, we do all the talking, and we don't take the time to listen to what the Lord wants to say to us. As we learn to be silent, the Holy Spirit will reveal the will of the Father to us.

Today, choose to forgive all those who have hurt and rejected you. You can become the very thing you hate if you don't forgive. Forgive others as Father has forgiven you. (See Ephesians 4:32.) Call on the name of the Lord and allow Him to shower you with His love. He wants to make you rejection proof, but you first have to lay your pain and anger at His feet.

Chapter Three: From the Pit of Retaliation to the Peak of Restraint

Points to Ponder

1. Joseph experienced the ultimate rejection, yet he remained rejection proof. How was he able to do this?

2. How did God bring blessing out of Joseph's pain? Can you see how He might do the same for you?

3. Putting up a wall is a common defense mechanism when facing rejection. Why is this method ineffective and actually harmful?

4. Have you ever felt angry when you have been rejected or not valued? How did you deal with your anger?

5. Reflecting on Psalm 4:4 and Ephesians 4:26, explain how it is possible to be angry and yet not sin.

Meditate on these Scriptures, speak them aloud, and commit them to memory.

Blessed is the man who perseveres under trial, because when he has stood the test, he will receive the crown of life that God has promised to those who love him. (James 1:12)

Be on your guard; stand firm in the faith; be men of courage; be strong. (1 Corinthians 16:13)

"In your anger do not sin": Do not let the sun go down while you are still angry, and do not give the devil a foothold. (Ephesians 4:26–27)

Do not repay evil with evil or insult with insult, but with blessing, because to this you were called so that you may inherit a blessing. (1 Peter 3:9)

— 4 —

FROM THE PIT OF BROKENNESS TO THE PEAK OF WHOLENESS

I finally found the love and acceptance I'd been longing for at the "Holy Roller" church down the road. God showed His love through the people in that little country church and used them to draw me into His kingdom.

Just as I did, everyone needs to feel loved, significant, and secure. In the garden of Eden, Adam and Eve enjoyed communion with God and harmonious union with each other, two types of relationships that totally fulfilled them. God met their every need: He fulfilled their need to feel significant by creating them in His image, and He fulfilled their need for fellowship and security by establishing their relationships with both Him and each other. (See Genesis 2:18.)

Adam and Eve's fellowship with God was broken, however, when they sinned. Satan, in the form of a serpent, deceived Eve and convinced her to disregard God's command and eat the forbidden fruit anyway. (See Genesis 3:1–6.) Satan told Eve, in essence, that she could find greater satisfaction living apart from God than from being with Him.

As a result, mankind's need for significance and security could not be met because their relationship with God had been broken—and their creation in His image had been distorted. They no longer had holy, intimate communion with God. In fact, they ran from it—Adam and Eve hid from God when they realized they were naked. (See Genesis 3:7–8.)

Thus, mankind searched to find significance and security in things other than God. To this day, people look to their careers, relationships, money, social positions, accomplishments, possessions, and other things to meet their God-given need for significance and security—but in vain.

Yet God provided a way for a restored relationship with Him through the sacrificial death and resurrection of His Son, Jesus Christ. When we come to Christ and accept Him into our hearts as Lord and Savior, He wants to be just that—Lord and Savior. He's not just our Savior who paid the price for the forgiveness of our sins so that we could spend eternity with God; He is also our Lord. Just as a landlord is in charge of his property, Christ wants to be in charge of our lives—precious "properties" belonging to the Father. At salvation, we also receive the gift of God's Holy Spirit into our lives. He enables us to follow Christ, and His presence is proof we belong to God. (See 2 Corinthians 1:21–22.) As we yield to Christ's lordship when we receive salvation, the Holy Spirit begins a work in us that is unlike anything that anyone else could ever do.

When we yield our hearts to Christ and accept His sacrifice on our behalf, our spirits are immediately "born again," bringing us back into union and communion with God. Once again, three of our needs—love, significance, and security—are found only in a relationship with God. And we can relate to God because, like Him, we are triune beings. God is a trinity of Father, Son, and Holy Spirits; similarly, we are spirits, we have souls, and we live in bodies. At the time of salvation, our spirits are born again, but our souls and bodies usually remain in the same condition until the Holy Spirit brings about His healing and deliverance in those realms, as well.

I call this process "unpacking the bags." It's a process that requires our willingness to yield continually to the Holy Spirit so that the broken areas of our lives may be made whole.

Unpacking the Bags

I travel a lot for my ministry, and I always seem to have at least one suitcase packed. I don't mind packing for trips as much as I mind unpacking afterward. Whenever my daughter, Destiny, and I return from a trip, I am left to unpack the bags—a process that I would rather not bother with. You're probably familiar with the steps—removing all the dirty clothes and washing them, putting other items away in their proper places, refolding every piece of clothing that came out of place, even if it wasn't worn, and then putting the suitcases back in storage until the next trip. I would much rather return home and forget about the bags.

We often have a similar attitude toward our spiritual and emotional lives—we'd rather not take the time to unpack our bags. The truth is, I had been on a long trip for seventeen years before I accepted Christ into my life, and I had a lot of emotional baggage traveling with me! I had to be willing to yield continually to the Holy Spirit as He assisted me in the unpacking process. And, actually, He did most of the unpacking. I had only to submit to what He wanted to do in my life.

Experiencing God's Unconditional Love

Again, the Lord used His people to love me into the kingdom of God and to keep me there when I easily could have gone astray. When I was saved, I was a senior in high school. I would go to church every Sunday and feel great, but, by Thursday evening, my friends would usually ask me to go out for the weekend. Each week, my Sunday school teacher would send me a little note letting me know that she loved me, that God loved me, and that she was looking forward to seeing me on Sunday morning. Her note would arrive just before I'd receive my friends' invitation to go out dancing. God's love—and His love that shone through my teacher—kept me seeking after righteousness at a time when the world was trying to pull me back.

My friends kept on asking me to join them, and, one weekend, I finally gave in to their persistent requests. I told the youth leader at church that I wouldn't be attending the weekly meeting. But God always had my number! On our way to a local nightclub, my friends and I were stopped at a traffic light where we'd turn in to the parking lot when I heard some loud music and joyful singing coming from the van next to us. As I glanced in that direction, I recognized the youth leader's van and immediately slouched down in my seat in an attempt to hide my face. Simultaneously, I heard a sweet, happy voice say, "Sister Danette—is that you? What are you guys doing tonight?"

"Oh, we're just driving around," I responded. Of course, the car's turn indicator made it clear where we were headed—the nightclub. The youth leader and the others in the van didn't yell at me, preach to me, or put me down. They just showed love to me and told me they were looking forward to seeing me at church on Sunday morning.

Needless to say, I felt convicted by the Holy Spirit the entire evening. It was that night when the Holy Spirit showed me that it was wrong for me to go to nightclubs. In the dark, smoke-filled room, I could sense an evil presence all around me. I could feel the guys looking at me with lust in their eyes, and I could see the demonic presence in the spirit realm. God opened my spiritual eyes that night to see in the Spirit, and I never went back!

God was opening my spiritual eyes not only to see the work of the enemy, but also to see the unconditional love of God. The thing that I had longed for, I now had. I knew I was loved, accepted, and valued—not only by my heavenly Father, but also by my new family: the family of God. The enemy had tried to destroy my family with the pain of divorce—my parents divorced when I was in fifth grade—but the Lord used His family, and His love through them, to bring healing and restoration to my life.

Walking in Love

When it comes to feeling significant and secure, love is the most important thing. The apostle Paul wrote, *"And now these three remain: faith, hope and love. But the greatest of these is love"* (1 Corinthians 13:13). In your relationships with other people, there's nothing more important than your love walk, which is the means by which you express God's love to others.

> *Dear friends, let us love one another, for love comes from God. Everyone who loves has been born of God and knows God. Whoever does not love does not know God, because God is love.* (1 John 4:7–8)

In order for us to walk in real love, God must be operating in our lives, for *"God is love"* (1 John 4:8, 16). When the Holy Spirit lives in us, we take on the nature of God, thus walking in love. Love is a fruit of the Spirit (see Galatians 5:22–23), and, unlike gifts that are given, fruit is *grown*. We have to allow the fruit of love to grow in our lives, and we have to cultivate it on purpose. We must actively develop our love walks on a regular basis. We can't "put on" or pretend that we are walking in love; rather, we must truly put on love by clothing ourselves with this most important fruit of the Spirit.

Love is to be desired above everything else. Love is *"the most excellent way"* (1 Corinthians 12:31). Without love, we are nothing, and we gain nothing. (See 1 Corinthians 13:1–3.)

The Father heart of God is filled with love for us, and His love is perfect. But what is love, exactly? And what is it not? Most of us grew up thinking love is just one of many emotions that we experience in life. But the Word of God gives us the real definition of love:

> THE FATHER HEART OF GOD IS FILLED WITH LOVE FOR US, AND HIS LOVE IS PERFECT.

> *Love endures long and is patient and kind; love never is envious nor boils over with jealousy, is not boastful or vainglorious, does not display itself haughtily. It is not conceited (arrogant and inflated with pride); it is not rude (unmannerly) and does not act unbecomingly. Love (God's love in us) does not insist on its own rights or its own way, for it is not self-seeking; it is not touchy or fretful or resentful; it takes no account of the evil done to it [it pays no attention to a suffered wrong]. It does not rejoice at injustice and unrighteousness, but rejoices when right and truth prevail. Love bears up under anything and everything that comes, is ever ready to believe the best of every person, its hopes are fadeless under all circumstances, and it endures everything [without weakening]. Love never fails.* (1 Corinthians 13:4–8 AMP)

Love is patient, and it endures long. Love is kind in words, in attitudes, and in nonverbal gestures. Love is never jealous or envious; so, when you are walking in love, you rejoice when others are blessed. Instead of acting out of jealousy, love says, "Me too, Lord. I know I'm next in line for my miracle!" In other words, you are excited for others when they receive blessings, and you know that God will bless you, too, for you are secure in His love for you. Love does not boast, and it is not vainglorious. The definition of *boast* is "to speak of or assert with excessive pride." When we boast or speak out of pride, our actions and words do not show love to those listening, who may end up feeling left out, unvalued, or inferior.

> *We do not dare to classify or compare ourselves with some who commend themselves. When they measure themselves by themselves and compare themselves with themselves, they are not wise.* (2 Corinthians 10:12)

The Word tells us that it is *not* wise to compare ourselves with one another. (See, for example, John 21:20–22; Romans 14:4.) God created us to be individuals—all different, but all equally wonderful. When you compare yourself with someone else, you come out feeling either superior or inferior. Neither of these feelings brings glory to the Father. When we feel superior, we step into pride—possibly even spiritual pride. When we feel inferior, we believe the lie that we have less worth or purpose than someone else, and we shrink back from stepping forward in faith. The only thing we should ever compare ourselves to is God's Word.

Evaluate Your Love Walk

To evaluate your love walk, ask yourself the following questions: *Do my thoughts, words, and actions line up with God's Word? How about my heart attitude and my obedience?* Comparing ourselves to God's Word gives us a clear reflection of who we really are. It reveals to us that which is motivated by our souls, apart from the influence of our regenerated spirits, and that which is motivated by our regenerated spirits. God's Word judges our thoughts and the attitudes of our hearts, and the Holy Spirit then reveals the truth to us like a mirror showing a clear reflection of truth. As the author of Hebrews wrote, *"The word of God is living and active. Sharper than any double-edged sword, it penetrates even to dividing soul and spirit, joints and marrow; it judges the thoughts and attitudes of the heart"* (Hebrews 4:12).

As we compare ourselves to the Word of God and follow His direction and desire for our lives, we yield to the leading of the Holy Spirit, who makes any necessary changes in our hearts and lives. But when we compare ourselves with others, we operate in the flesh by trying to conform to the way our flesh wants to be—like others or a false version of ourselves, and not like God.

One year, I attended an annual event at my local church. The sky was overcast, and it looked as though we were going to have a thunderstorm any moment. Destiny and I were both starving because it was two o'clock in the afternoon, and neither of us had eaten lunch. I had to make a judgment call. *Should we stay for this outdoor event in hopes that the weather will clear and we will be able to eat as planned? Or should we make a mad dash up the street and grab some lunch?*

While I was trying to decide what to do, Destiny begged me to stay with a quite dramatic appeal. I finally gave in. By now, not only was I starving, but I was also a little on edge. Finally, we were able to eat lunch, but then Destiny wanted a snow cone. Looking up at the sky, I decided to grab a snow cone and make a run for the car before it started to pour. The line at the snow cone machine wasn't particularly long, so I reasoned, *We can wait. At least Destiny won't be disappointed.* Seconds later, a young boy came out of nowhere and cut in line right in front of me. I was so upset—almost outraged. Then, I saw my attitude. I immediately thought to myself, *You have just reached an all-time low in your love walk.* I was allowing myself to be stressed out over unimportant things while overlooking the most important thing of all—my love walk. Not to mention the fact that I was at a church event, and the target of my anger was an innocent ten-year-old!

Practice Healthy Self-Love

In order to walk in real love with others, you first need to personally experience and accept God's unconditional love for you. If you don't love yourself as God's precious child or have a revelation of His love for you, it will be impossible to love others in the way Christ intends.

For you created my inmost being; you knit me together in my mother's womb. I praise you because I am fearfully and wonderfully made; your works are wonderful, I know that full well.   (Psalm 139:13–14)

Because we have been fearfully and wonderfully made by our heavenly Father, we can appreciate our individuality and love ourselves in a healthy way. The above passage tells us that it was God who knit each of us together in our mothers' wombs. No one is an accident, and you are no exception. God is the giver of all life, and He designed you with a particular plan in mind.

> BECAUSE WE HAVE BEEN FEARFULLY AND WONDERFULLY MADE BY OUR HEAVENLY FATHER, WE CAN APPRECIATE OUR INDIVIDUALITY AND LOVE OURSELVES IN A HEALTHY WAY.

I always say that to walk in true peace, we must be at peace with God, with ourselves, and with others. Our peace and our love walks are closely connected. If we don't have peace, it's extremely difficult to walk in love. And we can't live at peace with God until we have surrendered our hearts to Him through receiving salvation and our daily lives to Him through our obedience to the leading of the Holy Spirit. If we don't have peace with God, we definitely can't have real peace with ourselves or with others.

If our lives are not yielded to the Lord, the battle within us—the fleshly nature fighting against the spirit—will prevent us from having internal peace. People who are not at peace with themselves can never live in peace with others or enjoy healthy relationships. A person who's been hurt will usually hurt other people, and a miserable person often likes to make others feel miserable, as well. This attitude prevents intimate, healthy relationships.

But when we are at peace with God through right relationships with Him, we can know His unconditional love for us. The acceptance of His love for us, and the acceptance of His wonderful works, enables us to live at peace with ourselves. We then can be at peace with who we are, how we look, how we feel about ourselves, and all other aspects of our lives. Then, and only then, can we live at peace with others.

> *Peace I leave with you; My [own] peace I now give and bequeath to you. Not as the world gives do I give to you. Do not let your hearts be troubled, neither let them be afraid. [Stop allowing yourselves to be agitated and disturbed; and do not permit yourselves to be fearful and intimidated and cowardly and unsettled.]* (John 14:27 AMP)

We can choose to allow ourselves to get agitated and disturbed with ourselves and with others—but we don't have to make that bad choice. By receiving the peace and love that Father provides for us, we can stop allowing painful, unsettling things to rule our lives. That peace comes as a result of our accepting Christ's love for us and expressing it to others.

Show God's Love to Others

> *There is no fear in love. But perfect love drives out fear, because fear has to do with punishment. The one who fears is not made perfect in love.* (1 John 4:18)

God's love for us is perfect and unconditional. And He never changes. He is *"the same yesterday and today and forever"* (Hebrews 13:8), so His love for us never changes, either.

People often change their minds. One day, their words and actions may say they love us, but the next day, they may communicate something different. God's love for us, on the other hand, is forever. People aren't perfect—only God is perfect. Imperfect love and unhealthy relationships result from people's imperfections. We are all products of our pasts, to a certain extent, and we know how to love only with the kind of love with which we have been loved. We should never point a finger in judgment at those who weren't able to love us the way that we needed to be loved. Only rejoice in Christ's unconditional love for you and make it your goal to love others the same way that Christ has loved you.

Experience the Security of Love

"Perfect love drives out fear" (1 John 4:18), but imperfect, unhealthy love creates fear. Dysfunctional love and broken covenant relationships produce fear. Codependent and emotionally dependent relationships encourage and enhance fear, but *"there is no fear in love"* (verse 18).

> *"You are my servant"; I have chosen you and have not rejected you. So do not fear, for I am with you; do not be dismayed, for I am your God.*
> (Isaiah 41:9–10)

Because Father has chosen us and has not rejected us, we don't have to fear. Rejection, whether it's real or perceived, opens the door for fear to enter our lives. However, *"God has not given us a spirit of fear, but of power and of love and of a sound mind"* (2 Timothy 1:7 NKJV).

Fear is definitely a spirit. If God hasn't given us the spirit of fear, where do you think it came from? It came straight from the pit of hell. Satan loves for God's children to be bound up in any and every kind of fear: the fear of failure, the fear of man, the fear of abandonment, the fear of rejection, and so forth. We need to allow the Holy Spirit to reveal and uproot any fear and get it out of our lives. We must operate in God's provision for us—His power, His love, and His sound mind. We have been given Holy Spirit power to overcome anything we face in life.

Father wants us to be free to love and to be loved. Jesus said, *"Love your neighbor as yourself"* (Luke 10:27). If you don't love yourself, you can't love your neighbor with the love of God, as He intends you to. And we can love ourselves in healthy ways only by knowing Christ's unconditional love for us.

Chapter Four: From the Pit of Brokenness to the Peak of Wholeness

Points to Ponder

1. If you are like most people, you have some emotional baggage. Do you know what type your baggage is? Are you ready to let God help you unpack your bags?

2. Have you ever experienced rejection? If so, how did it make you feel? Did it change how you looked at yourself?

3. God loves you unconditionally. What keeps you from loving others the way He loves you?

4. Read 1 Corinthians 13:4–8 and evaluate your love walk. Do your thoughts, words, and actions line up with God's Word?

5. What is the importance of healthy self-love, and how can you practice it? What are the benefits of feeling loved by God?

Meditate on these Scriptures, speak them aloud, and commit them to memory.

There is no fear in love. But perfect love drives out fear, because fear has to do with punishment. The one who fears is not made perfect in love. (1 John 4:18)

God has not given us a spirit of fear, but of power and of love and of a sound mind. (2 Timothy 1:7 NKJV)

For you created my inmost being; you knit me together in my mother's womb. I praise you because I am fearfully and wonderfully made; your works are wonderful, I know that full well. (Psalm 139:13–14)

Let us love one another, for love comes from God. Everyone who loves has been born of God and knows God. Whoever does not love does not know God, because God is love. (1 John 4:7–8)

—5—

From the Pit of Aimlessness to the Peak of Purpose

After getting saved, I immediately started hungering for the things of God. I had gone from making fun of the "Holy Rollers" at that little church to thinking, *I'm the biggest Holy Roller here!* I really got radical for the Lord (and I believe we should all stay radical). I kept feeling like the Lord wanted to use me to travel and tell others about Christ. Out of my limited understanding, I thought I was going to be a truck driver for Jesus! After all, that was the only occupation I could think of that involved traveling all the time. (Remember, I grew up in the country!)

One weekend, the pastor announced that a guest speaker would be coming to our church. He was an evangelist, and he was to hold a revival there. I didn't know what an evangelist was, but I somehow knew the term *revival* involved a series of services. When I attended the services, I knew that God wanted me to do what this man did—travel as an evangelist, telling people about God and preaching His Word.

It took me a while to digest the idea, and the enemy lied to me for a couple of years before I really stepped into my calling. Although I was a straight-A student in high school, there was one class that I did not like— oral communication. The thought of standing before people and talking was extremely overwhelming. On days when an oral presentation was due, I would sit there shaking, wringing my hands together and wiping my sweaty palms, while I anxiously thought to myself, *I'll go first to get it over with. No, I'll wait in hopes that I'll be last.* I would get myself in a big tizzy over it!

When the Lord started speaking to me about working for Him, I began to rationalize why I couldn't do certain things. I imagined that I would probably marry a minister, and that was why I was feeling this call from the Holy Spirit. My mind was plagued with so many lies the enemy had told me over the years that I was "boxed in" to believing that I had many limitations. In a last-ditch effort to convince the Lord that I could never preach, I said, "But Lord, I'm a woman!"

He immediately responded, "Don't you think I know that? I'm the One who made you."

Out of my hunger for the things of God and my love for Him, I began taking small steps to follow His will for my life. I became a youth minister in my home church, with about five young people in my youth group. I thought, *Okay, five people—I can handle that.* I would study the Word and teach the young people on the weekends, but I made sure that I remained in my comfort zone.

Good-bye, Comfort Zone; Hello, Potential Zone

After graduating from high school, I requested to live with my father in an attempt to build the relationship that I had never had while growing up. I thought, *I'm a Christian now. I need to forgive my father.* I knew what I needed to do, but I didn't know that continually choosing to walk in forgiveness would be so difficult.

I didn't feel like I really knew my father, and I wanted to get to know him. After I moved into his home, we enjoyed long conversations and shared things about ourselves that the other never knew. I discovered that my dad felt that he, too, had been robbed of the joy of being around me while I was growing up, just as I felt I had been robbed of the joy of his presence. We shared a lot, cried a lot, and enjoyed spending the summer together.

In the fall, I started college at the University of Maryland. The academics were easy for me, but the hard thing was living with a bunch of college kids who weren't interested in learning about or serving God. This shocked me. I didn't join them, but I spent a semester cleaning up after kids who threw up all over the place as a result of their daily drinking habits. My pastor back home told me about a Christian school named Lee University in

Cleveland, Tennessee. *A Christian university?* I thought. *I never knew there was such a thing.* I immediately felt that this was where the Lord wanted me to attend college.

When I returned home after that first semester at the University of Maryland, my dad informed me that his girlfriend was moving in with us. *His girlfriend—living with us?* I was far from being a Bible scholar, yet I knew this was not right in God's eyes.

I will never forget the night I confronted my dad on this issue. I said, "Dad, I'm a Christian now. If I stay living in your home while you are choosing to live with a woman you're not married to, my actions would say that I'm in agreement with your decision." I proceeded to tell my father that if his girlfriend didn't move out, I would have to. Needless to say, he became very angry and told me she wasn't going anywhere. He also said that if I moved out, he wouldn't pay for any of my college education.

With tears flowing down my cheeks, I said, "Dad, I don't know what God has for my life, but I know He wants me to go to college. I'm sorry that you feel this way, but I know God will provide for me if I do the right thing."

The pain in my heart was great as I packed my belongings and moved back to my mom's house. I got two jobs and enrolled in the local community college full-time. This would be my first of many lessons about a truth God would teach me throughout the years to come: You must get out of your comfort zone to come into your potential zone. And out of my comfort zone I was!

If you are serious about coming into the full potential of what God has for you, you'd better make up your mind to kiss your comfort zone good-bye. No one comes into his potential zone unless he first gets out of his comfort zone—no one!

In the Old Testament, Abraham needed to get far from his comfort zone to come into the blessings God had for him. In Genesis 12:1, the Lord told Abraham, *"Leave your country, your people and your father's household and go to the land I will show you."* Talk about getting way out of your comfort zone! God was requiring Abraham to leave not only the place that was familiar to him—a place that gave him a sense of security—but also the people to whom he had been emotionally attached, even those upon whom he had been dependent. In order to obey God, he was to go to a land that was unfamiliar to him—and he wasn't even certain where he was going.

Then, after God challenged Abraham to leave his comfort zone, He gave him a glimpse of his potential zone. He said, *"I will make you into a great nation and I will bless you; I will make your name great, and you will be a blessing"* (Genesis 12:2). In other words, God was saying, "This is your potential zone. Will you kiss your comfort zone good-bye in order to embrace your potential zone?"

> WHENEVER WE CHOOSE TO LEAVE OUR COMFORT ZONES AS AN ACT OF OBEDIENCE TO GOD, WE CAN TAKE COMFORT IN THE JOY OF OBEDIENCE.

The choice to leave our comfort zones is always ours to make, and, each time we are faced with that choice, it's a little unnerving. But whenever we choose to leave our comfort zones as an act of obedience to God, we can take comfort in the joy of obedience. Later, we can reflect on all the blessings that came into our lives on the other side of our obedience—outside of our comfort zones.

Avoiding Detours and Distractions

Many people intend to set out for their potential zones but never arrive there because they get wrapped up in distractions that never allow them to take the first step—leaving their comfort zones. Others take that first step, only to fall for a detour somewhere along the way. A distraction can be a momentary diversion that quickly blossoms into a full-blown detour.

Over the years, my heart has broken time and again to see ministers lose everything as a result of taking a detour. Many church leaders have used their gifts and talents for the kingdom of God and have become very successful, only to fall for detours designed by the enemy to destroy them, their families, their ministries, and the congregations that the Lord had entrusted to their care. None of us is above falling into sin and compromise, of course, and we must be aware of the enemy's schemes. We must follow Peter's exhortation:

> *Be self-controlled and alert. Your enemy the devil prowls around like a roaring lion looking for someone to devour. Resist him, standing firm*

in the faith, because you know that your brothers throughout the world
are undergoing the same kind of sufferings. (1 Peter 5:8–9)

We should never flirt with detours but seek to follow the leading of the Holy Spirit. You flirt with detours by entertaining or meditating on thoughts that are opposed to what God has told you to do. Many times, we ask for others' opinions on things. We want to see what they think about our situations. In reality, we know what we should do because God already told us, but we are trying to talk ourselves—and let others talk us—into doing something different. We are trying to get a second opinion—the one we really want to hear. Opinions from family members and friends are just one type of detour that may reroute us back to our comfort zones.

Don't flirt with a detour, because the results can be devastating. Many people never arrive at their potential zones as a result of detours. Abraham, on the other hand, set out for Canaan—his potential zone—and arrived there because of his complete obedience.

Maybe you are off on a detour today. Maybe you have been there for several years, and, as a result, your life is a mess. The good news is, all you have to do is repent and ask the Lord to forgive you. When we confess our sins to God and repent, God not only forgives us, but He also lovingly leads us out of the detour and places us back on the highway headed to His purposes and plans for our lives.

The Distraction of Relationships

Sometimes, relationships can serve as distractions that threaten to keep you from entering your potential zone. Abraham had to separate himself from his nephew, Lot. (See Genesis 13:5–12.) After he did, he began to see his potential zone clearly. Not everyone around you sees your potential zone. And, you can't always see your potential zone with everyone around. Just as Abraham had to separate himself from Lot before seeing all that God had for him, you may have to separate yourself from those who represent sin and compromise in your life in order to embrace your potential zone. I can tell you from firsthand experience, you will be glad you did. Moreover, others will be blessed by your stand for righteousness.

The Distraction of Intimidation

When Nehemiah determined to rebuild the wall around Jerusalem, he faced great opposition from the enemy. (See Nehemiah 4–6.) Yet he still chose to embrace his potential zone. When the enemy came to intimidate and distract him, Nehemiah remained focused. He set out to rebuild the wall, and he did it!

As we pursue our potential zones, the enemy will recruit people, situations, and circumstances to mess with our plans and try to send us scurrying back to our comfort zones. He did with Nehemiah, and He will with us. We need only to respond the way that Nehemiah did.

> *Sanballat and Geshem sent me this message: "Come, let us meet together in one of the villages on the plain of Ono." But they were scheming to harm me; so I sent messengers to them with this reply: "I am carrying on a great project and cannot go down. Why should the work stop while I leave it and go down to you?"* (Nehemiah 6:2–3)

Every time the enemy tries to send you a message of distraction, give him the *same* answer: "I don't have time for you. I'm pursuing my potential zone!"

In Your Potential Zone, You Come Closer to God—and Must Trust Him like Never Before

As I said, I knew the Lord wanted me to attend Lee University, so I set my eyes upon the goal that the Lord had set before me. I worked extremely hard to keep my grades up, and I earned an academic scholarship. In between my full-time load of courses at the community college, I worked two part-time jobs to pay for my education and cover other expenses.

Through all this, I began to witness God's miraculous provision as I sought to fulfill His will for my life. The words I had tearfully spoken to my dad on the night I'd decided to leave his house had become a reality— my heavenly Father provided everything I needed for college. As a young Christian, I hadn't fully understood what I'd said that night—it had just come out of my spirit. The very thing that I had once resented—having to stand in faith for God's provision—proved to be a vital requirement from the Lord in order to build my life. God really does work all things together for our good. (See Romans 8:28.) He sees the big picture, and He's in control of every area of life, whether we realize it or not.

After I had served faithfully for several years as the youth minister at my church, the Lord began to open new doors for me. I transferred to Lee University as a junior and became active in various ministries on campus. My Father's hand of favor was forever extended to me as He wonderfully provided for my every need.

> MY FATHER'S HAND OF FAVOR WAS FOREVER EXTENDED TO ME AS HE WONDERFULLY PROVIDED FOR MY EVERY NEED.

Up until this time, I had been driving a beat-up little Volkswagen Bug. But, hey, it was God's provision! When my grandmother found out that I was going to attend college in Tennessee, she bought me a used car to assure my safety during the thirteen-hour trip that I would be making regularly for the next two-and-a-half years. My grandmother always believed in meeting the need, and God used her in my life during moments of great need. She taught me by example that it really is more blessed to give than to receive.

It was during the next two years that God gave me a clear vision concerning my call to ministry. Leaving home to attend a college thirteen hours away was challenging; the University of Maryland had been close enough for me to go home on weekends. I can still remember taking my mom to the airport for her flight home after visiting me at Lee. While heading to my car after walking her to her gate (you could do that back then), I looked up and said, "Well, God, it's just You and me now." I would soon learn that it was an awesome place to be—alone with God.

Chapter Five: From the Pit of Aimlessness to the Peak of Purpose

Points to Ponder

1. What do you have to kiss good-bye if you want to come into your potential zone?

2. Many people set out to do God's will in their lives but never actually fulfill it. What was it about Abraham that enabled him not only to set out to do God's will, but also to accomplish it?

3. What are some of your comfort zones? Are you willing to leave them behind, like Abraham was?

4. What distractions are keeping you from arriving at your potential zone?

5. Why do you think God wants you to make it to your potential zone?

Meditate on these Scriptures, speak them aloud, and commit them to memory.

And we know that in all things God works for the good of those who love him, who have been called according to his purpose.

(Romans 8:28)

Yet the LORD longs to be gracious to you; he rises to show you compassion. For the LORD is a God of justice. Blessed are all who wait for him!

(Isaiah 30:18)

Teach me to do your will, for you are my God; may your good Spirit lead me on level ground.

(Psalm 143:10)

So we fix our eyes not on what is seen, but on what is unseen. For what is seen is temporary, but what is unseen is eternal.

(2 Corinthians 4:18)

—6—

From the Pit of Deception to the Peak of Truth

During the year or so before getting saved, I had been depressed. Everything that I had suppressed during my childhood had begun to surface, and I hadn't known how to deal with it. As I sought to take steps forward in God's plan for my life by attending Lee University, the devil kept trying to lie to me. Before I moved to Tennessee, Satan would whisper in my ear, "You're going to get down there and fall into a deep depression again." The depression that I had experienced earlier was awful. It felt like I was in a deep, dark hole and couldn't get out.

Well, Jesus had gotten me out, and I was determined that I was never going back in. But I had to identify the lies of the enemy, rejoice in the truth of God's Word, and continue to proceed forward in God.

Know Who You Are in Christ

One of the first things that the Lord began to heal me from was the way I thought and felt about myself. He began to show me who I was in Christ—I had never known!

In John 10:10, Jesus said, *"The thief comes only to steal and kill and destroy; I have come that they may have life, and have it to the full."* When the enemy is able to steal, kill, and destroy in our lives, we cannot experience the abundant life that Christ has ordained for us to have. Again, one of the schemes that the enemy uses to bring about great destruction in our lives is deception. Let's take a look at how Jesus described the devil's nature:

He was a murderer from the beginning, not holding to the truth, for there is no truth in him. When he lies, he speaks his native language, for he is a liar and the father of lies. (John 8:44)

The enemy spoke his native language to me for many years, and, for a while, I believed the lies. They were designed to disable me from proceeding forward. They were intended to stop me in my tracks, to paralyze me with the devastating emotional pain of his deception.

Praise God—He began to identify the lies that were ruling and controlling my life, including the lie that no one loved me, the lie that I was ugly, the lie that no one cared about me, and the lie that I was worthy of rejection. The more I studied God's Word, the more truth I learned. The more truth I learned, the freer I became.

To the Jews who had believed him, Jesus said, "If you hold to my teaching, you are really my disciples. Then you will know the truth, and the truth will set you free." (John 8:31–32)

Again, the key word in this Scripture is *know*—it's the truth you *know* that will set you free. Truth can't set you free unless you know the truth. And, you must know it in your heart and in your spirit, not just in your mind as head knowledge. This is a process that the Holy Spirit performs in our lives. As we allow the Lord to identify the devil's lies, the Holy Spirit can uproot the deception that might otherwise have grown into a stronghold.

Don't Buy the Lie

I want to encourage you today—don't buy the lie! Maybe the devil has tried to sell you a bunch of lies over the course of your life. Well, don't buy the lies any longer. Maybe there are lies that you have believed for many years. Maybe there are little lies that the enemy throws at you every now and then in his attempt to discourage and distract you. Make a decision today to allow the Holy Spirit to uproot the lies, and then don't buy them as truth for another minute!

There have been times in my life when I was just going about my day, doing what I needed to do, when, all of a sudden, I got an overwhelming feeling of discouragement, fear, or anxiety. Whenever this happened, I would stop and ask myself, *Why am I feeling this way? I was having a great day.* The Holy Spirit has taught me over the years to stop and identify the lie that was operating in that moment. In doing this, I was able to trace the lying thought back to something simple, such as words that someone had said to me, a thought I had entertained about a situation, or some unexpected news I had received. As we go back to the root of the lie, we can speak God's Word to the situation or circumstance and immediately take authority over it.

Again, God's Word tells us to bring every thought captive and make it obedient to Christ. (See 2 Corinthians 10:5.) The thoughts we have about ourselves, the thoughts we have about others, and the thoughts we have about situations and circumstances must line up with God's Word if they are going to produce good fruit in our lives. If we don't study God's Word, we won't know the truth when we are confronted with a counterfeit argument from the enemy.

When individuals who work with money are being trained to identify counterfeit currency, they study the real thing. They don't study the counterfeit; they study what a real twenty-dollar bill and a real hundred-dollar bill look like. If they are schooled in what a true bill looks like, they can spot a counterfeit quickly and easily. The same is true for us as God's children. When we study the real truth, the Word of God, we can identify Satan's counterfeits a mile away. We can identify the lie and quickly rejoice in the truth of God's Word.

Don't live with the lie. Identify it and get rid of it. Don't embrace the lie like it's a member of the family, and don't be consumed by it. We need to be consumed with the report of the Lord and not the report of anyone else. The enemy loves for us to sit around and obsess over things spoken to us, about us, or by us. To *obsess* is "to haunt or excessively preoccupy the mind." Never allow the enemy to harass you or preoccupy your mind with words that were spoken.

Remember King Jehoshaphat? He received some alarming news, yet he didn't obsess over the words spoken to him. After he and the people of Judah inquired of the Lord through fasting and prayer, the word of the Lord came forth. God's response, as delivered by a man named Jahaziel, is recorded in the book of 2 Chronicles:

Listen, King Jehoshaphat and all who live in Judah and Jerusalem! This is what the LORD says to you: "Do not be afraid or discouraged because of this vast army. For the battle is not yours, but God's."

(2 Chronicles 20:15)

Jehoshaphat didn't buy the lie—don't you buy it, either! The lie was that the army of Judah would be destroyed by this vast army that was coming against them. Just like Jehoshaphat, when we are confronted by a lie, especially when it's easy to believe, we need a word from the Lord. His Word is truth, and we need to be preoccupied with His Word alone about every situation.

Not only was the army of Judah victorious, but God fought the battle for them! *"After consulting the people, Jehoshaphat appointed men to sing to the LORD and to praise him for the splendor of his holiness as they went out at the head of the army, saying: 'Give thanks to the LORD, for his love endures forever'"* (2 Chronicles 20:21).

Like Jehoshaphat's appointed men, we rejoice in the truth after we've identified the lie. As the appointed men praised and worshipped God, they focused on God's report of the situation. We need to let the evil deeds of darkness (the lies of the enemy) be exposed by the light (God's Word). And as we do, we will be set free from the "box" that Satan's lies have placed us in for many years.

Beginning to Be Pulled Out of the Box by the Rope of Hope

During my college years, God performed a great deal of emotional healing in my life. While at Lee University, I accepted the call to preach, even though I still didn't understand how it could be. *Me, preach?* I thought.

When I arrived in Cleveland, Tennessee, I got a job to assist in paying for my living expenses. Although I had an academic scholarship, I still had plenty of expenses to cover. As I stepped out in faith to attend Lee, an amazing (or should I say miraculous?) thing happened. My dad changed his original verdict on the matter of finances and informed me that he would begin helping me—but only for the next two years.

> GOD WAS TEACHING ME THAT IF I JUST DID WHAT HE TOLD ME TO DO, HIS PROVISION WOULD BE THERE. THE DOUBTS THE DEVIL HAD PLANTED IN MY MIND STARTED TO DISAPPEAR.

Wow! God was teaching me that if I just did what He told me to do, His provision would be there. The doubts the devil had planted in my mind started to disappear. Attending school in Tennessee was a giant step of faith, and it cost a lot more than the community college back home did. But I took that step of faith, and God did the rest. He even dealt with my dad's heart. My dad later made things right before God and got married. God was teaching me to take a stand for righteousness, no matter what the cost!

Because of my dad's financial support and my mom's weekly cards filled with fives and tens, I was able to quit my job in Cleveland and focus on my class work and on ministry. I joined the evangelism team at Lee, and we traveled to different churches to minister just about every weekend. We also traveled in the summer and during school breaks. I was asked to be the treasurer, and I consented—because, after all, that position was in my "comfort zone." (I was an accounting major for two years before changing to counseling.)

As I traveled with the evangelism team, God continually stirred in my heart the call to minister. I would hear a word from the Lord, and I would tell the young men on our team what God was saying. Then, they would go and preach my revelations for me. This happened on several occasions. God lovingly allowed me to stay in my comfort zone long enough to get me to the place where I was willing to get out of the box I was in.

Coming Further Out of the Box

During spring break one year, we traveled to a church in Shawnee, Oklahoma. The entire team was excited, and we had awesome services, but I was still in my "box" working as the treasurer. The pastor announced that every team member would be sharing a ten-minute message in the pulpit—kind of a tag-team preaching night. I was nervous, but I thought, *Ten minutes—I can handle that.*

Little did I know that God was gently and lovingly getting me out of my box. That night, I ended up preaching my first message. I spoke about the body of Christ being one body with many parts, based on Paul's teaching in 1 Corinthians 12:4–31. Although I didn't know it at the time, I was preaching not only to the congregation, but also to myself!

At the end of the week, all of the young men on our team were hoping to be asked back to preach at a weeklong revival. Much to their surprise—and mine, as well—the pastor asked me to come back to do a weeklong revival. *Me?* The men were the preachers on the team; I was just the treasurer. *For a week?* Hey, I could handle ten minutes, but a week?

After much debate, I consented to return to *teach* for a week—not preach. I didn't realize it at the time, but this invitation to do a weeklong district youth revival was really quite an honor. I didn't really know what that was, but all the guys on the team did, and they wanted the opportunity!

A few months later, at the beginning of the summer, I returned to that church in Oklahoma for my weeklong "teaching." By this time, I was quite excited. I would study the Word of God all day and teach all evening. After the service, I would eat a quick meal with the pastor and his family before returning to my room to study. The next morning, I would wake up before anyone else and go next door to the church, where I'd spend the day with the Lord, fasting and studying.

Something began to happen to me during this daily routine. I would take a break from studying every afternoon and go into the sanctuary to pray for the evening service. During my prayer times, I began preaching to the empty pews with a boldness that I had never experienced before. Honestly, I yielded to the Holy Spirit only because I knew no one was there to see or hear me. Then, in the evenings, I would calmly teach the Word to the people who filled the pews that had been empty just hours earlier. By the end of the week, it was all I could do to remain calm as I taught the Word. It was as though a mighty, rushing river was trying to break loose, and I was trying to keep it back with a dam that seemed to be cracking. I didn't know at the time that this is exactly what was happening. The river of God wanted to flow through me, and I just needed to yield my will to it.

> THE RIVER OF GOD WANTED TO FLOW THROUGH ME, AND I JUST NEEDED TO YIELD MY WILL TO IT.

At the end of my weeklong teaching, the pastor asked me to stay an extra day and attend a special service the next night. I agreed. At the end of the service, the minister asked people to come forward for prayer. As I approached the front of the church, I said, "Lord, if this is really You, if You have really called me to preach, I'll do it. I just need to know for sure."

I'd looked around the room during the service, and the place was filled with a majority of men who were in the ministry, all of them much older than I. I'd felt intimidated by this earlier in the service, and while I was at the altar praying, I brought up the fact once again. Immediately, God showed me a vision. I saw myself in the palm of His hand. It was as though the Lord winked at me and said, "But you are My little girl!"

My mom had had a miscarriage before becoming pregnant with me, and the doctors had been concerned that she was going to lose me, too. I remember thinking then that the fact that I'd made it was significant. Something inside of me knew that, from my mother's womb, I had been called to ministry.

Confirmations of My Calling

When I returned home, my phone started ringing. People were asking me to come and speak at their churches. My initial response was, *Who told you I was called to preach?* Until this point, I had never mentioned it to anyone. It was only between the Lord and me. Well, God heard my prayer. I had said that I needed to know for sure, and He was making it obvious not only to me but to others, as well.

Whether I liked it or not, I was getting out of the box. I have to admit, the thought of getting out of my comfortable box was actually much more frightening than the act of getting out itself. And once I got out, I never wanted to go back!

Sure, there were a few uncomfortable moments—take my first real revival, for example. I had practiced my message several times, and it was about forty-five minutes long. But in front of the seemingly massive crowd of sixty-five people, I completed the message in a nervous twelve minutes. I spoke so fast that it sounded like I was speaking in tongues. I was embarrassed, and the thought of returning for the remaining four nights made me feel faint. But I kept in mind what the Lord told me when I'd asked Him how I was going to preach. He said, "Just get up there and do it."

Well, that's what I did. I just got up there and did it—one step of obedience at a time. And that's what I have been doing ever since! When I obeyed God and defied Satan's lies, which told me that I couldn't preach, couldn't teach, couldn't lead, I found favor and success.

Chapter Six: From the Pit of Deception to the Peak of Truth

Points to Ponder

1. The lies of the enemy are designed to disable you. What has this chapter taught you about identifying the devil's lies? List some ways you can do this.

2. Make a list of some of the lies that the devil has spoken to you about yourself and then make a list of what God says about you.

3. How have the lies that the enemy has spoken to you personally disabled you?

4. Do you know who you are in Christ? How does knowing enable you to be victorious over the works of the devil?

5. If you know the truth, you can easily spot a lie. What can you do to keep the enemy from preoccupying your mind with lies?

Meditate on these Scriptures, speak them aloud, and commit them to memory.

The devil…was a murderer from the beginning, not holding to the truth, for there is no truth in him. When he lies, he speaks his native language, for he is a liar and the father of lies.   (John 8:44)

The thief comes only to steal and kill and destroy; I have come that they may have life, and have it to the full.   (John 10:10)

If you hold to my teaching, you are really my disciples. Then you will know the truth, and the truth will set you free.   (John 8:31–32)

We demolish arguments and every pretension that sets itself up against the knowledge of God, and we take captive every thought to make it obedient to Christ.   (2 Corinthians 10:5)

—7—

From the Pit of Self-Direction to the Peak of Obedience

Hearing the voice of God is easy. It's walking in obedience to do what He's told us to do that's hard—hard on our flesh, that is. God requires our obedience, not our understanding. We don't have to understand why God is telling us to do or not to do something; we have only to obey. There are always blessings waiting for us on the other side of our obedience.

In the book of 2 Chronicles, we read about Hezekiah, who prospered because of his obedience and his hard work. *"In everything that he undertook in the service of God's temple and in obedience to the law and the commands, he sought his God and worked wholeheartedly. And so he prospered"* (2 Chronicles 31:21).

Keys to our prosperity are obedience and hard work. Sometimes, it's hard work to walk in obedience. God wants to bless us in every area of our lives. He wants to bless us with His peace, joy, and contentment. Father wants to bless us with physical health and financial blessings. God's Word tells us that we will be blessed going out and coming in (see Psalm 121:8 NKJV), but our disobedience can tie the hand of God and hold back our blessings.

Abraham received the promises of God because of his faith and obedience. (See Hebrews 11:8–12, 17–19.) The same can be true for us today. As we step out in faith, doing what the Lord tells us to do—whether in His Word or as He prompts our spirits—we can walk in obedience and step into all that our heavenly Father has for us.

Moving On in Obedience

My years at Lee University were great, and by my last year, I was ready to go win the world for Jesus. I knew my call, I was somewhat out of the box, and I was tired of studying. Because I loved Cleveland, Tennessee, so much, my plan was to keep my base there and travel full-time as an evangelist. The key phrase here is "my plan." We often get a sense of security from having everything all mapped out. But, over the years, I've learned not to plot my own course too specifically, because I know I'm wasting my time. I know now that the Lord will reveal His plan to me in His timing and not an hour earlier.

The book of Proverbs conveys this truth several times over, perhaps most concisely in Proverbs 16:9: *"In his heart a man plans his course, but the LORD determines his steps."* After I would spend months "planning," the Lord would come to me during my prayer time with what I call a big "Holy Ghost eraser" and remove all of my plans in a single moment.

Obedience Requires Faith

Father's direction became very clear to me as I approached graduation. I knew without a shadow of a doubt that I was to attend graduate school at Regent University in Virginia Beach, Virginia. I was back in the same boat all over again—trusting God and walking by faith. I have come to learn that the boat of total faith and trust in God is really the best boat I can be in. It isn't always a comfortable boat, but it's the best boat.

Though my dad had reminded me that his generous contributions toward my college education would end upon my graduation from Lee, I stepped out in faith and applied to Regent University. Soon, a telephone interview was scheduled.

During the interview, the person reviewing my application commented, "Is this correct? Your savings and checking accounts are both at a zero balance? You don't have any support from family or outside sources, and you don't have a job?"

At this point, I was extremely glad that this was a telephone interview. Had it been face-to-face, I would have been crawling under the carpet at this point. "Yes, uh...that's correct, sir," I answered. I had completed the form he was reviewing just weeks earlier. On the right-hand side of the form was a list of all the expenses I would have as a graduate student—tuition, books, rent, utilities, food, etc. And on the left-hand side were all the sources of possible income. On my form, the right-hand side was filled with astronomical figures; the left-hand side was filled with zeros—all zeros! I said to myself, *This guy's going to think that I'm crazy.*

"How do you plan on paying for graduate school?" he asked.

I mustered up all the strength I could and, through quivering lips, answered, "I'm not exactly sure, sir. I only know that the Lord is telling me I'm supposed to go."

I was extremely surprised to hear him say, "Well, if God's telling you to come, you'd better come."

I continued taking steps of faith toward attending graduate school. After being accepted, I was met with another pleasant surprise. I received an academic scholarship for my first year, which would be renewed automatically for the second year as long as I maintained a 3.8 grade point average (GPA). God was doing it again—His hand of provision met me at every step of obedience.

Next, I needed to buy my books, pay my rent, and eat. I could eat cheaply—I was experienced at that! With a graduation gift of one thousand dollars in hand, I set out for my new home in Virginia Beach. Once again, I knew no one, but this time, I had already gotten a little practice in getting out of the "box."

Obedience Requires Ignoring the Enemy's Lies

Looking back, I know now that when I arrived in Virginia Beach, I had only begun to get out of the box. I had allowed the Lord to rip open the top, and I had one leg hanging out! But to get all the way out of the box would take a little more time.

Perhaps you are like I was at that time. You have been in a box and may expect to stay there. Maybe you've even put yourself in a box. Perhaps other people have issues that they've taken out on you—through abuse, for example—and this has boxed you in. Maybe you are boxed in because you have allowed others to put you there with their words or actions. No matter how you got there, God is saying that it's time to get out of the box and obey Him.

We can become boxed in when we believe lies from the enemy. Unfortunately, it's all the fears attached to the lies that keep us there. Maybe you are boxed in today as a result of believing a lie. Here are some lies to watch out for:

+ *No one loves me.*

+ *No one cares about me.*

+ *I am rejected, and I'll never be accepted.*

+ *I don't have what it takes to succeed in life.*

+ *I don't have enough education.*

+ *I wasn't born into the right family.*

Now, that's a list of lies! When you begin to renew your mind by the truth and combat the lies, you allow God to rip open the box. Just when you are really thinking about getting out, that's when the enemy tries to pull you back with all the fears he has attached to those lies. The fear of failure, the fear of rejection, the fear of man, and sometimes even the fear of success are designed to keep us in boxes all of our lives.

It's the lies of the enemy that put us in the box, but it's God's truth in His Word that sets us free from the box. When we allow God to uproot the lies by the power of His Holy Spirit, all of the fears attached to the lies must go, as well. Lies open the door for fears, but when you identify the lies and no longer accept them as truth, the fears attached to the lies will no longer have power in your life.

Obedience Requires Absolute Trust in God's Provision

As I was attending graduate school, I worked a couple of part-time jobs and continued traveling as an evangelist. I would waitress during the week, scrape together all of my tip money on Friday evenings, and fill up my gas tank early on Saturday mornings before driving to whatever revival I was scheduled to preach at that weekend. I worked at a family-style buffet restaurant to avoid having to serve any type of mixed drink. As a result, my tips kept me living by faith—and I'm not exaggerating one bit!

Over the years, I came to the conclusion that one of the best means of training for ministry is working as a server, for it demands that you give your customers your very best, no matter what you receive in return. I learned that if I served and did everything *"as working for the Lord"* (Colossians 3:23), He would provide for me. However, His provision wouldn't necessarily come from the source I'd thought it would.

God was doing so much in my life that it was hard to keep up. For the first time, the academics at my school were challenging for me, so I learned how to rely on the Holy Spirit more than ever. The Word tells us that the Holy Spirit leads us and guides us into all truth. (See John 16:13.) The Holy Spirit is called "Counselor" and "Teacher," and the Bible says that He will bring all things back to our remembrance. *"But the Counselor, the Holy Spirit, whom the Father will send in my name, will teach you all things and will remind you of everything I have said to you"* (John 14:26). This verse refers to what Jesus has said to us, but I found that the principle also applied to any academic exams for which I studied. Now, if I didn't study, I couldn't expect much help. But, if I did my part, the Holy Spirit taught me that He'd do His part in bringing all things back to my remembrance.

The Lord was faithful, and, in spite of my busy schedule, He enabled me to maintain a GPA of 3.8, which meant that my scholarship was renewed for a second year. I eventually quit my part-time jobs and traveled as an evangelist just about every weekend. God miraculously provided for me, and I graduated debt-free. I didn't have ten cents to my name, but I didn't have any debt, either. I learned God's provision at a whole new level, and God was teaching me to live with a standard of excellence in all areas of life.

Obedience Brings Fulfillment

God's purpose in bringing me to the Virginia Beach area was multifaceted. Upon arriving in Virginia Beach, I was delighted to find a role model in another woman in ministry. Up until that point, I hadn't had one. My new pastors would prove to be an important element in my ministerial training. I had never met anyone who walked by faith like they did. They set a great example, and, through their ministry, God took me to a whole new level in the Word, as well as in the things of God.

The day after I graduated from Regent University, I left for a three-month road trip. I traveled for the entire summer from church to church, holding revivals and special meetings. After returning to Virginia Beach in the fall of 1989, I established Joy Ministries and continued traveling full-time.

The next two years were both powerful and fulfilling; they were unlike anything I had ever experienced before. I was functioning in my call full-time, and there's nothing greater than that. God taught me to be myself. He showed me that I was anointed when I was just myself; I didn't have to be like anyone else. If I tried to be like this one or that one, I wouldn't be anointed. But when I sought God and allowed the Holy Spirit to use me, the power of God would move in a mighty way.

> GOD TAUGHT ME TO BE MYSELF. HE SHOWED ME THAT I WAS ANOINTED WHEN I WAS JUST MYSELF; I DIDN'T HAVE TO BE LIKE ANYONE ELSE.

In the story of David and Goliath, when little David tried to use someone else's armor, it didn't work. But when he reached for his slingshot and stones, the giant came down in a single shot. (See 1 Samuel 17:38–50.) Likewise, as I followed David's example by being myself, the giants began falling for me.

After I had spent two years traveling, the Lord spoke to me and said, "I want you to go home and serve your pastors." I thought He meant for a few months, but, much to my surprise, it ended up being several years. I took a position on the staff at my local church and continued traveling as an evangelist.

God said to me one day, "You are half-baked. I'm going to put you back in the oven." I understood that He meant I was going to be completely prepared for ministry, but I didn't fully realize the details at the time. He was putting me back in the oven, but He was also about to turn up the heat. My pastor liked to call this your "necessaries." "Everyone who goes into the ministry must go through his 'necessaries,'" he would say. In other words, you must totally die to your flesh in every area of life for the anointing to increase in your life. It wasn't a fun time, but it was fruitful.

If given a choice, most of us would rather take an elevator than climb a steep set of steps. We like to get on the elevator, push a button, and arrive at the top in our workplaces, our schools, and our ministries with as little effort as possible. But there are great benefits to our physical health by taking the steps because doing so gives us a workout. The same is true in other areas of our lives. The steps are important because we learn vital lessons every step of the way. As a result, the Lord usually leads us toward the steps rather than the elevator. No one who expects to grow takes the elevator but rather the steps.

> The steps of a [good] man are directed and established by the Lord when He delights in his way [and He busies Himself with his every step].   (Psalm 37:23 AMP)

Our steps are ordered by the Lord, and the Lord has placed our steps in a certain order for a reason. It reminds me of the game called connect the dots that children like to play. Every one of our steps is a dot on the page. When all you can see is a bunch of dots, it doesn't make any sense to you. But when the Holy Spirit begins to connect the dots, you can clearly see the beautiful picture that the Lord is making. Not only does the Lord order and direct our steps, but He also "busies Himself" with our every step. In other words, God makes our every step His business! We may not understand why a certain step is important, but when God connects all the dots, the picture will become crystal clear. We need only to obey Him by taking steps of faith.

Chapter Seven: From the Pit of Self-Direction to the Peak of Obedience

Points to Ponder

1. God requires our obedience, not our understanding. Why do you think this is so?

2. There are always blessings on the other side of obedience. Give an example of some "obedience blessings" that you have received.

3. What three things does obedience require, as discussed in this chapter?

4. How does knowing who you are in Christ enable you to be victorious over the works of the devil?

5. What personal choice can you make today to keep the enemy from preoccupying your mind with lies and keeping you trapped in a box?

Meditate on these Scriptures, speak them aloud, and commit them to memory.

If you are willing and obedient, you will eat the best from the land.
(Isaiah 1:19)

The steps of a [good] man are directed and established by the Lord when He delights in his way [and He busies Himself with his every step]. (Psalm 37:23 AMP)

In his heart a man plans his course, but the LORD determines his steps. (Proverbs 16:9)

Trust in the LORD with all your heart and lean not on your own understanding; in all your ways acknowledge him, and he will make your paths straight. (Proverbs 3:5–6)

—8—

From the Pit of Denial to the Peak of Progress

After a few years of working on the church staff and traveling, I was assigned to a special project that our church was doing, and the senior pastor put me in charge of the event. It was during the preparations for this event that I met the man I would later marry. He was handsome, with gorgeous, blue eyes and a personality that kept everyone laughing. We dated for over a year before getting engaged, then got married after a six-month engagement. As any young bride's, my heart was filled with hopes and dreams of spending the rest of our lives together and building a family.

Immediately after we got married, however, I realized that my husband had portrayed an image to me of the person that he really wanted to be—but wasn't. The first night of our honeymoon, he verbally abused me—something he'd never done before. Off and on, I would catch him lying to me, telling me what he knew I wanted to hear. It concerned me greatly, yet I was determined to work through every challenge that we faced. His verbal and emotional abuse continued, but it was sporadic, and I kept thinking that if I could be the "perfect" wife, everything would be all right.

After about two years, I began to figure out that something was seriously wrong in our marriage. I had never been married before, and I didn't know what constituted a "normal" sexual relationship between a husband and wife. My husband worked nights a lot, and I worked at the church during the day. I gave him the benefit of the doubt over and over again because of our conflicting schedules, yet I still wondered, *Why isn't he more interested in sleeping with me?*

I questioned his behavior on numerous occasions because he didn't seem to be interested in me the way a husband should be interested in his wife. I confronted him several times about his possible involvement in pornography, but he denied it every time. He usually proceeded to get very angry and verbally abusive. He had this unique way of pointing the finger at me and saying that everything was my fault. He would call me a jealous, possessive wife, yet he continued to show little to no interest in me sexually.

Turmoil overtook my mind. Whom could I possibly talk to and confide in? I was traveling as an evangelist and serving on the staff at a large local church. What would people think if they knew about the problems we were having at home? What if I went in for counseling, and others in the church found out? What would my husband's response be if he knew I had discussed this with someone? My mind was plagued with questions that I did not know the answers to, and I didn't know where to turn.

Most of the time, when we don't know what to do, we do nothing. After doing nothing for an extended period of time, we resort to denial in an effort to survive the difficult situation. Denial is a disowning or a refusal to believe or accept something. I didn't realize it at the time, but denial was my coping mechanism from early on in my marriage. I was so far in denial after two years that it took a lot for the Lord to shake me out of that place of internal deception.

The Defense Mechanism of Denial

As children, we often don't know how to handle painful emotions, so we develop defense mechanisms in our carnal attempts to survive difficult circumstances.

JESUS HEALS OUR WOUNDS WHEN WE TAKE THEM TO THE CROSS.

When we try to ignore or contradict the facts, we practice what's known as denial. Denial is a defense mechanism that will never get us anywhere. Whatever our problem, no matter how deep our pit, we must feel it and deal with it. We must allow ourselves to feel even unpleasant painful emotions—but then we take them to the cross and let Jesus heal our wounds.

The book of Isaiah says that Jesus *"was pierced for our transgressions, he was crushed for our iniquities; the punishment that brought us peace was upon him, and by his wounds we are healed"* (Isaiah 53:5). By His wounds, we are healed—spirit, soul, and body. Jesus died on the cross for us to be healed not only spiritually, but emotionally and physically, as well. Like many people, I was never taught this truth as a child. I was an adult before I knew that Jesus wanted to heal me of all of the emotional brokenness in my life. It is true—the enemy tries to put us in a pit at a young age, and he wants to keep us there for the rest of our lives.

I want to emphasize that things are different when you aren't a child any longer. You can make choices and decisions that may not have been available or conceivable to you as a child. I would have to accept the truth of my husband's problem in order to deal with it.

Awakened to Reality

After two years of marriage, I conceived my daughter, Destiny Joy. It was a moment in my life for which I had waited many years. In January 1997, Kim Clement had prophesied over me and said that God was going to open my womb. He'd said that I would conceive a little girl who would be a worshipper and love to dance before the Lord. His word gave me great hope, as I had suffered prior complications in becoming pregnant. The day I received the exciting news of my pregnancy, I immediately ran home to tell my husband.

I was determined to enjoy every day of my pregnancy because, after all, I had waited for this time to come for many, many years. The nine months of my pregnancy proved to be the best of times and the worst of times—the best of times for obvious reasons, the worst of times as unpleasant surprises kept surfacing.

In my third month of pregnancy, I was relieved from my duties at the church without explanation, leaving me without a salary or health insurance. At the time, this change seemed to be a big storm in my life; however, I later realized that God was actually positioning me to weather the biggest, most devastating storm that I would ever go through.

During my sixth month of pregnancy, the Lord revealed truths to me that started to shake me out of my state of denial. My suspicions grew as my husband continued to show little interest in me physically. Night after night, morning after morning, he would sit at the computer for hours. I would go downstairs, sometimes in the middle of the night, only to find him on the computer in a chat room communicating with various women. Every time I questioned his behavior, he would attempt to intimidate me by calling me a jealous, possessive wife. And his attempt to intimidate me with verbal abuse worked. His angry words caused me to refrain from posing any additional questions because I wanted to keep the peace. All along, I kept thinking, *If I am just the perfect wife, everything will be okay.*

After I learned how to access his frequently visited Web sites, my suspicions were confirmed—my husband was addicted to pornography. My world was shattered, not only by his addiction, but also by his habitual lies to cover it up. Although I was temporarily shaken from my state of denial, I returned to my mind-set of refusing to accept or deal with the reality of his addiction. After all, I was six months pregnant and thought, *This can't possibly be happening to me!* I had served God for all of my adult life, I had given myself totally to the Lord and His work, and I had waited years to have a daughter. I didn't have the time, the energy, or the knowledge to deal with the giant called pornography—not to mention the overwhelming sense of rejection I was feeling.

Sunshine in the Midst of the Storm

The remaining months of my pregnancy passed quickly. I was supposed to be due at the end of June, but by the Fourth of July, my stomach still seemed bigger than life—and so did the mounting problems at home. My husband continued to deny his involvement with porn, even after he learned about the discovery I'd made on his computer.

On July 4, yet another bomb was dropped. My husband informed me that he had planned on leaving me nine months earlier. The day I'd come home with the news of my pregnancy, he had planned on giving me the news that he was leaving. He proceeded to tell me that he had stayed with me only because I was pregnant, but his intention was still to leave me. I was devastated. It was just days prior to the delivery of my daughter, and he was telling me this?! I wanted to go home where my family was, but how could I? My doctor was here. Whom could I talk to? What should I do? I felt so alone and so devastated.

On July 9, my bundle of joy arrived. She was truly my sunshine in the midst of the storm. God was so gracious to me. My labor and delivery were smooth, and I dilated seven centimeters without feeling any real pain. I delivered my daughter in only five hours, and I can honestly say that I enjoyed every minute of it. I was surrounded by family and friends who shared my excitement, and I have great memories that I will always cherish. However, I was left without an answer when the nurses asked, "Where is your husband?" This wasn't something new. I had been asked questions over the past few years that had me continually covering for my husband—questions for which I didn't have answers.

On Sundays: "Why isn't he at church?"

At holiday celebrations with family: "Why isn't he with you?"

And now, in the delivery room: "Where is your husband?"

Although he was there for the actual birth, he left a short time later. I was so embarrassed. There I was, still in the delivery room, and my husband had somewhere else he needed to be. Yet I continued to cover up for him in the hopes that everything was going to be all right—if I'd just become the perfect wife.

Reality Hurts, but It's Better than the Numbness of Denial

In the first two weeks after returning home with my new bundle of joy, I was surrounded by the gifts and love of family and friends. Shortly afterward, I was again shaken from my state of denial. This time, I experienced the final jolt into reality that I desperately needed. As more information surfaced, the proof was devastating. My husband was not only addicted to pornography, but he also had a sexual addiction that extended further.

As things escalated, our home became an unsafe place for both my daughter and me. Although I knew my husband would never intentionally hurt Destiny, his altered state of mind was continually proving dangerous. After I confronted him with the truth that he, too, was desperately trying to run from, he began drinking heavily. He would return home intoxicated with his gun in hand. Finally, he moved out, and I was left in the place where I had always said I never wanted to be—the place of a single mom.

> I SOON LEARNED THAT GOD AND I TOGETHER WERE THE MAJORITY, AND AS LONG AS GOD WAS STANDING WITH ME, THAT WAS ALL THAT I NEEDED.

Emotionally, I felt like the scenes you see on the news of a town after a tornado comes through. The only thing standing is the doorframe of a basement, and the rest of the house looks like a pile of toothpicks. I felt like my life had been shattered into a pile of toothpicks, and the only thing left standing was me with a little baby and a great, big God. I soon learned that God and I together were the majority, and as long as God was standing with me, that was all that I needed.

Chapter Eight: From the Pit of Denial to the Peak of Progress

Points to Ponder

1. Define denial and explain why you think we find ourselves using it to cope with difficult situations.

2. Has there ever been a time in your life when you were in denial? What were you trying to cope with?

3. How do dealing with reality and facing the facts help you to make progress?

4. In this chapter, we learned that we have to allow ourselves to feel the pain in order to deal with it. But, after we feel the pain, what must we do to get healed?

Meditate on these Scriptures, speak them aloud, and commit them to memory.

But he was pierced for our transgressions, he was crushed for our iniquities; the punishment that brought us peace was upon him, and by his wounds we are healed. (Isaiah 53:5)

Cast all your anxiety on him because he cares for you. (1 Peter 5:7)

My grace is sufficient for you, for my power is made perfect in weakness. (2 Corinthians 12:9)

And the God of all grace, who called you to his eternal glory in Christ, after you have suffered a little while, will himself restore you and make you strong, firm and steadfast. (1 Peter 5:10)

—9—

FROM THE PIT OF SELF-PITY TO THE PEAK OF CONTENTMENT

I have to admit, being a single mom is the hardest thing that I have ever done. But I can honestly say that I know God in a more intimate way than ever before. I took comfort in the truth of Isaiah 54:5: *"For your Maker is your husband—the LORD Almighty is his name."* My Maker, my heavenly Father, has been my Husband every step of the way. I actually have the best Husband I could ever have.

Talk about a good provider—my Husband owns it all, and He meets all my needs! (See Philippians 4:19.) Talk about loving me unconditionally and thinking I'm beautiful—He's the one who made me "fearfully and wonderfully," just like He wanted me! (See Psalm 139:13–16.) And what about protecting me? My Husband sends me forth each day with an angelic escort that's so much better than even a police escort! (See Psalm 34:7.) So, what do I have to whine about? Nothing! I may be single, but I am definitely not alone.

Destiny was only two months old when my husband moved out. I was dealing with all the normal emotions that a woman deals with after the birth of a child. I was adjusting to caring for an infant because this was my first child, and, on top of all this, I was separating from my husband.

Because my family lived five hours away, opportunities for them to help me with my daughter were few and far between. Daily, I had to choose to go forward. Daily, I had to release the old in order to embrace the new. I had to focus on caring for my daughter and giving her a safe, stable home. With my newborn baby and my great, big God, I had to refuse to feel sorry for myself.

107

I had to renew my mind daily with God's Word, and I had to refuse to have any pity parties. I didn't have time for them. Did I think about pity parties? Yes. I even bought the invitations and sent them out. But, by the grace and mercy of God, I cancelled the party before anyone had time to show up.

Shortly after my husband and I separated, the Lord nudged me to invest in myself by going to professional counseling. He miraculously provided, and I received the counsel that I needed. I believe that everyone can benefit from professional, godly counseling. It helped me sort things out and see the truth. I learned that addicts always blame others for their problems—it's a part of the denial that keeps them trapped in their addictive behaviors.

My husband finally did go for a few counseling sessions but then refused to go anymore. Sure enough, he claimed that everything was my fault and that he didn't have any problems. The verbal and emotional abuse that I had lived with had caused me to believe that everything was my fault, that if I could just be the "perfect" wife, everything would be okay. I needed to come completely out of my denial and see things in a clear, healthy light. I needed to deal with my own issues and brokenness, as well.

Releasing the Old, Embracing the New

For the first year, I hung on to the hope that we would get back together. I fasted often and prayed practically nonstop for the restoration of our marriage. I lost so much weight that I was down to 107 pounds just months after my daughter was born. I did everything that I could do, yet my husband slipped further and further away from God and our family.

One day, as I was arriving at a Joyce Meyer conference, I felt that the Lord gave me this message: "You have to release the old so I can bring the new into your life." I knew right away what God was saying. He was telling me that my husband and I were going to be divorced. The thought really hadn't been anywhere in my mind up until that time. I had been standing in faith and believing God for total restoration, and I felt almost as shattered that day as I had on the day we got separated. I had to face the fact that I was going to go through a divorce and would be a single mom.

Arise [from the depression and prostration in which circumstances have kept you—rise to a new life]! Shine (be radiant with the glory of the Lord), for your light has come, and the glory of the Lord has risen upon you! (Isaiah 60:1 AMP)

The road to my recovery wasn't an easy one, nor was it a short one. But the good news is that God brought me through, and He will bring you through, too. There were many days when I was so emotionally devastated that I couldn't even hold my head up. I can remember other days when I was so excited that I had met my goals for the day— taking a shower and putting on makeup. Believe me, that was a big accomplishment for someone who was hanging on to life by only a fingernail.

> GOD BROUGHT ME THROUGH, AND HE WILL BRING YOU THROUGH, TOO.

After crying for about nine or ten months and just trying to survive everyday life, I heard the Lord say, "Get up out of your mess and go do what I've called you to do." In other words, He was saying, *I have given you time to grieve, and now you have to move on.*

Move On

After the death of Moses the servant of the Lord, the Lord said to Joshua son of Nun, Moses' minister, Moses My servant is dead. So now arise [take his place], go over this Jordan, you and all this people, into the land which I am giving to them, the Israelites.

(Joshua 1:1–2 AMP)

The law of Moses allowed the Israelites thirty days to mourn. After those thirty days, the Lord told Joshua to arise and take his new position. It was time to move on! Joshua had to release the old in order to embrace the new.

When faced with times of sorrow and disappointment, we must release the old so that we can step forward to embrace all the things that Father has for us in the future. When God told Joshua that Moses was dead, He was basically saying, "Release the old." He went on to say, "*Now arise.*" Don't stay stuck where you are; arise—and arise now!

Joshua had to learn how to handle new responsibilities, and he may not have felt ready. Well, that's where faith and total dependence on God come in. We don't have to feel ready, nor do we have to be comfortable, to be obedient to the Lord. Actually, most of the time, our flesh is not comfortable when we are taking a step forward, because, again, we always have to get out of our comfort zones in order to come into our potential zones.

Leave the Past Behind

The Lord had challenged me to move on, yet, as desperately as I desired to move on, I daily had to make choices to release the old. Like Joshua, I had a mountain of new responsibilities that I didn't feel like handling. I'd become a single mom with a newborn daughter overnight, and I had no income—none.

Many times, we choose to stay in an old place even after the Lord has said, "It's time to move on." Our decision to hang on to the old is usually rooted in our sense of security—a *false* sense of security, I might add. Some people stay in harmful, dangerous situations because they say their children need their mother or their father. All children need healthy, safe homes filled with love. The ideal is to have that type of home with both parents happily married, but that can be impossible when one parent or the other refuses to seek help. I have been comforted over the years by knowing that God is truly a Father to the fatherless.

As the Lord prompted me to release the "old"—the depression and prostration in which my circumstances had kept me—I had to choose daily to embrace the "new"—my new life with the Lord and my daughter. Father continually told me that His plan for me hadn't changed—I was to shine and be radiant with the glory of the Lord as I fulfilled the call He had on my life.

My call hadn't changed. God's love for me hadn't changed. And He reminded me constantly that He and I together were the majority. It doesn't matter what anyone else thinks, and it doesn't matter what anyone else does. You and God together are the majority, too!

Seed Your Own Need

Let us not become weary in doing good, for at the proper time we will reap a harvest if we do not give up. (Galatians 6:9)

The first few weeks and months of divorce challenged me in every area. During this time, I developed a new saying: "Life is hard, but God is good." I quickly learned that the harder life became, the more God's grace and mercy were extended to me. Yes, my life was harder than I had ever experienced it to be, but the presence, love, and goodness of God were shown to me daily like never before.

One day, while I was driving down the street past my home, the Lord said to me, "Seed your need and know where to sow." He was revealing to me an important biblical principle that would enable me to come successfully through the battle I was in.

The principle of reaping and sowing, as established by the Lord, is summed up in Galatians 6:7: "*A man reaps what he sows.*" In other words, every seed produces after its own kind. Tomato seeds produce tomatoes. Apple seeds produce apples. Orange seeds produce oranges.

When we sow encouragement into others' lives, we reap encouragement in our own lives. When we sow hope into others' lives, we reap hope in our own lives. When we sow financial seed on good ground, we reap a financial harvest in our own lives. We reap whatever we sow. The Lord began to teach me to get my eyes off of myself and what I was going through. He said clearly to me, "There's always someone hurting worse than you are. There's always someone who has been through more than you have." It was into the lives of those individuals who were suffering more than I was that I began to sow my time and finances. I began to actively look for women who were in great need.

One night, between ten and eleven o'clock, the Lord prompted me to go to the prayer room at my home church. Usually, I was never out that late, but the Lord was ordering my steps. I was praying in the prayer room; Destiny was with me in her baby carrier. At one point, I got up from praying to go to the restroom, and I noticed a woman in another part of the prayer room, sobbing uncontrollably. I went over to her and began to minister to her. As it turned out, she was in an abusive marriage, and her husband had just beaten her. I was so blessed to be able to sow encouragement, love, and hope into her life.

This became a regular thing for me—the Lord would bring women across my path, and I would "sow" into their lives, simultaneously "seeding my own need." It was amazing—as I encouraged them, *I* became encouraged. As I shared hope with them, *I* became filled with hope. God took me back to the days when I'd first begun preaching and reminded me of something He'd told me as I was ministering at my first few revivals. He'd said, "Keep your eyes on Me and your heart on the needs of My people." Nothing had changed except my circumstances, and I couldn't allow my circumstances to cause me to get stuck on "self" focus.

As time passed, the Lord continued to heal my heart and minister to many, many women through me. One day, the Lord revealed to me that there were single moms living only two to three miles from the church who didn't know how they were going to feed their children dinner that night. All the years that I'd sat in my "cushy, cushy" office at the church, I'd never known that there were single moms in need mere miles away. There's nothing like firsthand experience to help us develop hearts of compassion for those in need. I didn't know how I was going to feed my daughter, either, but I *did* know who my Provider was—my Husband, the Lord God Almighty.

I began taking groceries to the single moms who lived in a subsidized housing development a few miles away. I would tell them about the love of Jesus and how He died on the cross for the forgiveness of their sins. I'd take just about everything I had in my pantry and give it to the moms in need in that neighborhood, and, every time I did, the Lord would prompt someone to leave a bag of groceries on my front porch! I was seeding my own need, and I was reaping an awesome harvest for Destiny and myself, as well as for the kingdom of God.

Persevering with Patience through Painful Times of Transition

A *transition* is defined as "passage from one state, stage, subject, or place to another." We are always transformed during times of transition. When Father transitions us from the old to the new, it can be a painful process. However, on the other side of a transition is a totally transformed person. When we reach the transformed stage, we will be glad that we went through the transition process, and we'll never want to go back to the way we were beforehand.

Welcome Transition as a Time of Transformation

God the Father forms us, and the Holy Spirit transforms us. *To transform* means "to change in composition or structure; to change the outward form or appearance of; to change in character or condition." After the storms we face in life, after the unexpected changes we go through, and after the unexpected transitions we face, we come out truly transformed— if we submit to the process. The caterpillar goes from a hairy worm to a beautiful butterfly because it experiences a total transformation, and the transformation takes time. If the cocoon is opened during the transition time, the caterpillar will die and never become what the Father intended it to be—a beautiful butterfly.

Help Others in Their Times of Transition

Times of transition usually aren't fun, but as we focus on the finish line and submit to the process, we can step into all that Father has for us. Transition, or change, almost always takes us out of our comfort zones. But, remember, we must say, "Good-bye, comfort zone" to be able to say, "Hello, potential zone." Father wants us to release the old so that we can embrace the new in our lives, and He wants us to help others do the same. He wants us to continue the work of Jesus, which is summed up in Isaiah:

> *The Spirit of the Lord God is upon me, because the Lord has anointed and qualified me to preach the Gospel of good tidings to the meek, the poor, and afflicted; He has sent me to bind up and heal the brokenhearted, to proclaim liberty to the [physical and spiritual] captives and the opening of the prison and of the eyes to those who are bound.*
>
> (Isaiah 61:1 AMP)

As God's children, we, also, are anointed and qualified to minister the gospel to others. Jesus qualified us when He went to the cross, and the only things that can disqualify us are our poor choices and our decisions—no one else's! So, we must keep our hearts right and our mouths shut. Before we know it, the transition time will be over, and we will have been transformed into the

AS GOD'S CHILDREN, WE ARE ANOINTED AND QUALIFIED TO MINISTER THE GOSPEL TO OTHERS.

beautiful people Father created us to be. Then, we can help others come through their transition times, too, as we share the gospel with them and offer our own testimonies to encourage them.

Coming through the Storm

As I said earlier, I had to make the choice to get up. That sounds easy—unless you feel so far down that you're not sure which way is up. That's where the Lord comes in. He will show us, one step at a time, one day at a time—we need only to choose to get up. We can't wallow in our self-pity; we can't meditate on how unfair life has been to us. We have to look up to the Lord, and we have to get up.

There are several reasons why we may find ourselves in the midst of storms in this life. A storm can be a result of our disobedience, someone else's disobedience, our lack of self-discipline, or even the gracious hand of God. But in the midst of the storm, the important thing is your survival, not the answer to the question, "Why is this happening to me?" God will reveal the "why" to us in His timing. Searching for the answer in the midst of the storm is as unwise and futile as searching outside for a favorite pair of shoes in the midst of a Category 5 hurricane—not smart, not important!

Guard Your Mouth and Heart

God taught me several keys to succeed in getting to the other side of my storm. The first thing the Lord told me was to keep my mouth shut and my heart right. The heart and the mouth are closely connected. Jesus said, *"Out of the abundance of the heart the mouth speaks"* (Matthew 12:34 NKJV), and Proverbs 4:23 instructs us, *"Above all else, guard your heart, for it is the wellspring of life."*

Our hearts are either the wellsprings of life, as God intends them to be, or the wellsprings of death. Sound confusing? Here is another Scripture to help you understand: *"The tongue has the power of life and death"* (Proverbs 18:21). The power of life and death is in my tongue, and out of the abundance of my heart, my mouth will speak. If my heart is not right—if I have anger, bitterness, and offense—my mouth will give voice to negative heart attitudes, thus speaking words of death and not of life.

Don't Nurse It, Don't Rehearse It; Just Curse It

The Lord spoke to me about hurts and said, "Don't nurse it, don't rehearse it; just curse it in the name of Jesus." Let me explain. When we "nurse it," that means we sit around, coddling our hurts and wounds with thoughts such as these:

+ *No one else has things as rough as I do.*

+ *Life just isn't fair.*

+ *Nobody loves me, everybody hates me, and I may as well go out and eat worms.*

Well, somebody else can go out and eat worms if he wants to, but worms don't sound very appetizing to me! The Word does say that we will *eat* the fruit of our words: *"The tongue has the power of life and death, and those who love it will eat its fruit"* (Proverbs 18:21). So, if we choose to talk continually about all the worms in our lives, then we need to be prepared to enjoy the taste of those worms.

When we rehearse the emotional hurts in our lives, we tell everything about our worms to anyone who will listen. We don't just tell about them once or twice; we repeat the same old, awful things we've been through, over and over and over again. Twenty years down the road, we're still shoving our worms down other people's throats by continuing to rehearse our hurts with our words.

But when we curse the hurts and wounds in our lives in the name of Jesus, we uproot the devastating effects of any stronghold that the enemy is trying to plant. When we take every hurt, every disappointment, and every rejection to the foot of the cross, we can walk freely in the forgiveness that we've offered to our offenders—the same forgiveness that Christ has extended to us. If we are going to get up out of our messes successfully, we must keep our mouths shut and our hearts right! Was that easy for me? No way. Was it worth it? Absolutely!

Abide in the Vine

The way to maintain a pure heart through the pits and peaks of life is by abiding daily in the vine—the True Vine.

I am the True Vine, and My Father is the Vinedresser. Any branch in Me that does not bear fruit [that stops bearing] He cuts away (trims off, takes away); and He cleanses and repeatedly prunes every branch that continues to bear fruit, to make it bear more and richer and more excellent fruit. You are cleansed and pruned already, because of the word which I have given you [the teachings I have discussed with you]. Dwell in Me, and I will dwell in you. [Live in Me, and I will live in you.] Just as no branch can bear fruit of itself without abiding in (being vitally united to) the vine, neither can you bear fruit unless you abide in Me. (John 15:1–4 AMP)

> WE CAN REMAIN IN THE TRUE VINE— WE CAN STAY IN GOD'S PRESENCE, SUBMIT TO HIS WORD, AND COME SUCCESSFULLY THROUGH EVERY STORM, WHATEVER THE SOURCE OF THE WIND AND RAIN.

If we aren't abiding in the True Vine, our lives will not bear the fruit of the Spirit—*"love, joy, peace, patience, kindness, goodness, faithfulness, gentleness and self-control"* (Galatians 5:22–23). Jesus is the True Vine, but there are many false vines that we can abide in, if we aren't careful. *To abide* means "to remain stable or fixed in a state; to continue in a place;...to accept without objection." We can remain in constant stress and turmoil, burned out by trying to figure out how in the world we are ever going to make it through the storm. We can choose to submit to the pressures and deal with our storms in worldly, ungodly, unproductive ways. Or, we can remain in the True Vine—we can stay in His presence, submit to His Word, and come successfully through every storm, whatever the source of the wind and rain.

We get the strength and nourishment of our lives from the vine that we are abiding in. Are we getting our strength, confidence, and emotional nourishment from abiding in something other than the Lord? When we abide in anything but the Lord, it is detrimental to our survival. When we abide in false vines, they produce false fruit in our lives, such as a false sense of security, a false sense of peace, a false sense of acceptance, and a false sense of self-importance. But when we abide in the True Vine, Jesus— through prayer, worship, and the study of His Word—we can produce great fruit.

If we let Him, God will use our storms to prune us so that we can be even more fruitful. What Satan means for evil, God will use for our good— if we only keep our hearts right. *To prune* means "to reduce especially by eliminating superfluous matter;...to cut off or cut back parts of for better shape or more fruitful growth." Father is the One who does the pruning, so we can stop blaming those around us—it's not them; it's God. Many people don't like to submit to the pruning process, and so they *become* prunes instead of *getting* pruned. They get bitter, angry, and spiritually dried up, just like a prune. I want to challenge you not to become a prune but to submit to the pruning process. Allow the Lord to produce great fruit in you and through you, even in the midst of your storms.

When I put the past behind me and refused to wallow in self-pity, the Lord healed my broken heart, reestablished healthy boundaries in my life, and showed me that the best thing I could ever do for my daughter, other than teach her about the Lord, was to be a healthy, whole mother who loved her. As a single parent, I have been able to teach her that the Lord is a Father to the fatherless, and that He is our Provider and Protector.

Chapter Nine: From the Pit of Self-Pity to the Peak of Contentment

Points to Ponder

1. Why is it absolutely essential to release the old before embracing the new?

2. Is there something from your past that the Lord is challenging you to leave behind?

3. If you are in need, whether financially or otherwise, perhaps God is calling you to "seed your own need." Can you think of someone whom you could reach out to and bless? What might you be able to do for that person?

4. Explain in your own words what is meant by the phrase, "Don't nurse it, don't rehearse it; just curse it." Why is this process so important?

5. What is one way to maintain a pure heart through the pits and peaks of life, according to our discussion in this chapter?

Meditate on these Scriptures, speak them aloud, and commit them to memory.

Arise [from the depression and prostration in which circumstances have kept you—rise to a new life]! Shine (be radiant with the glory of the Lord), for your light has come, and the glory of the Lord has risen upon you! (Isaiah 60:1 AMP)

Finally, brothers, whatever is true, whatever is noble, whatever is right, whatever is pure, whatever is lovely, whatever is admirable—if anything is excellent or praiseworthy—think about such things. (Philippians 4:8)

Let us not become weary in doing good, for at the proper time we will reap a harvest if we do not give up. (Galatians 6:9)

Forget the former things; do not dwell on the past. See, I am doing a new thing! Now it springs up; do you not perceive it? I am making a way in the desert and streams in the wasteland. (Isaiah 43:18–19)

—10—

From the Pit of Doubt and Despair to the Peak of Trust and Hope

Our hope comes from whatever we are trusting in. If I am trusting in a paycheck, my spouse, or child support to take care of me, the day will probably come when that trusted thing or person will fall through, resulting in a loss of hope. If I am trusting in people to meet my emotional needs, the day will probably come when they let me down, and I lose my source of hope. Don't get me wrong—we need to trust people, but we don't need to trust *in* people. We need to trust in the Lord alone. When we trust in Him, our hope is in Him, and we are filled with unconditional joy and peace. Even when we wake up in a pit, we have peace in the pit, because our hope is in the Lord.

What we put our trust in will determine how much time we spend in the pit and what our experience there will be like. When we trust in the Lord, we'll have strength not to quit, and we'll have peace even in the midst of the pit. We can never forsake fellowship with the Father while we are in circumstances that are "the pits." It's His presence and power that encourage us in the pit.

Financial Strain Plants Seeds of Doubt

It was a fall day, and the weather outside was beautiful. The leaves were beginning to change, and they displayed a variety of colors. However, the atmosphere inside our small, cozy home was quite different. It was the last day of the month, and tension was mounting as I faced the realization that my monthly mortgage payment was due the next day.

During this new season in my life—single motherhood—financial pressures were great. Not only did I have the responsibilities of caring for an infant 24-7; I was also shouldering the financial responsibilities of our household alone. The court date my husband and I had set had been delayed time and time again as he repeatedly avoided the scheduled hearings. It took several months for the terms of his child support payments to be set, and even after an amount had been decided, his payments were unpredictable and unreliable for quite a while. I returned to court two or three times to have the court order enforced to prevent further delinquent child support payments.

Each month following my separation from my husband, I worked hard at walking in total obedience to the Lord, who had told me to get up out of my mess and do what I'd been called to do. I was willing to obey, but what about all my financial responsibilities? Child support wasn't enough to meet all of our needs, so we were walking by faith, with or without it.

As I was seeking to walk in obedience to my heavenly Father, I would say, "Okay, God, I know it's Your will for me to pay my bills and to pay them on time." In my mind, though, I doubted, and I'd brainstorm about backup plans. I'd think to myself, *If I can't pay my bills this month, I'm going to get a secular job.* I had earned a master's degree in counseling that I could have fallen back on, but I definitely didn't want to work as a counselor. I had enough of my own problems. *I can see it now,* I thought. *Someone will walk into my office with her "little" problem, and I will want to slap her, because what I've been going through has to be a lot worse than her current situation.*

So, I knew that counseling probably wouldn't work. I actually wanted a "no-brainer" job—one that would allow me to work my scheduled hours and leave at the end of the day with no pressure following me home. I thought, *I know—I'll go work at Wal-Mart!* I love to talk to people, and I wanted to be the person who stood at the door, passing out stickers and saying, "Thank you for shopping at Wal-Mart, thank you for shopping at Wal-Mart."

Every month when my mortgage was due, I'd threaten God. I'd say, "Okay, God, if this is Your will for me—to keep doing what I'm called to do—then, all right. But if I can't pay my mortgage this month, I'm going to work at Wal-Mart." Yet, every month, the Lord came through. It might have been at 11:00 p.m. on the night before my mortgage was due, but the Lord always put the money in my hand.

Because the Lord miraculously provided the money for my mortgage payment every month, it was obvious to me that I was in His will. I would think, *I'm not going to ever doubt again. I'm not going to ever bring up the idea of going to get a secular job.* Yet, as the first of each month approached, I would slowly begin to waver. Honestly, it took me about two years to get over the wavering and to just know that my mortgage would be paid.

> GOD WAS PATIENTLY BUILDING MY FAITH AND TRUST IN HIM—FAITH AND TRUST THAT I WOULD NEED TO FULFILL HIS CALL ON MY LIFE.

God was so patient with me, even though I wasn't patient with Him. I didn't like how the provision always came at the midnight hour. I would complain and worry—all for nothing. God was patiently building my faith and trust in Him—faith and trust that I would need to fulfill His call on my life.

Some months, the Lord would tell me to go to a certain person and ask him or her to make my mortgage payment. I would have to humble myself and go ask. Other months, the Lord wouldn't allow me to ask anyone for help. I don't know which was worse—asking for help or not being able to mention the issue to anyone. Both situations were extremely humbling in their own ways.

One lady at my church used to ask me, "Danette, do you need anything?" The only thing the Lord would allow me to say in response was, "Yes, I need diapers." I would then think, *Lord, I need a lot more than diapers!* But I quickly learned that Father wanted my obedience because He was doing a great work in my heart.

Doubt Your Doubts and Face Your Fears

The Lord spoke to me one day and showed me that I was filled with all kinds of fears—fears with deep roots since my childhood. He said, "If you are going to fulfill the call I have on your life, you must doubt your doubts and face your fears."

It's true that I was filled with a lot of doubt. I doubted that I could continue to minister because I was now a divorced, single mother with a newborn daughter. I doubted that we could make it financially. I doubted this, and I doubted that.

The Lord began to remind me that the devil is *"a liar and the father of lies"* (John 8:44). So, everything the devil was telling me was exactly opposite of the truth.

God told me, "You need to doubt those doubts." So, whenever a doubt would come into my mind, I would simply say out loud, "I doubt that! I know God is going to provide. I doubt that! I know God's going to fulfill His call on my life." It worked. Faith began to grow in my heart, and the doubts slowly faded.

Again, Proverbs 18:21 says, *"The tongue has the power of life and death, and those who love it will eat its fruit."* We can speak life or death to our faith and our emotions with our own words. Start speaking the Word of God over yourself and all that pertains to you, and faith will arise within your spirit.

After doubting my doubts, I had to face my fears. When you've doubted your doubts, you can take a step of faith and face your fears in order to begin to take action.

The first of my fears God dealt with was the fear that I wouldn't be provided for. While I was growing up, my father wasn't present as a provider. My mother struggled to provide for my brothers and me, and I was very aware of the financial pressures she faced daily. Plagued by stress and anxiety, my mother would discuss financial matters openly in front of us children, and, as I've said, I grew up worrying about money.

Children aren't prepared to handle adult pressures, such as finances, nor should they have to be. Children should know only that Father will provide. Even in single-parent homes, the children should be taught that their heavenly Father will provide for their every need.

When I was growing up, I didn't have a personal relationship with the Lord, and neither did my mother. She didn't know anything about our heavenly Father's provision for His children. So, our family, like many others, lived with great financial pressure and no assurance of provision.

As the Lord began to put His finger on the root of this fear in my life, He lovingly assured me that He would provide for my needs. One day, while

GOD LOVINGLY
ASSURED ME THAT
HE WOULD PROVIDE
FOR MY NEEDS.

sitting on my bed and looking out my window, I gazed up at the beautiful, passing clouds and began to pray. Immediately, the Lord responded to my prayer concerns about our financial needs. He said, "It's nothing for Me to take care of your little girl, your little house, and your little self."

Wow! Father had spoken! And He was reassuring me that He would provide for us. He was putting things into perspective for me. It was nothing to my great, big God—the God of the universe—to provide for my daughter and me. We were just specks in this world, and it was nothing to God to provide for our little needs. The needs that seemed so big and overwhelming to me were really small to God. He was basically saying, "Consider it done!"

The years that followed proved to be exciting, as I witnessed firsthand my Father's miraculous provision. I had to choose daily to allow this faith walk to be exciting and not overwhelming. We have the choice, you know!

Jesus said to his disciples: "Therefore I tell you, do not worry about your life, what you will eat; or about your body, what you will wear. Life is more than food, and the body more than clothes. Consider the ravens: They do not sow or reap, they have no storeroom or barn; yet God feeds them. And how much more valuable you are than birds! Who of you by worrying can add a single hour to his life? Since you cannot do this very little thing, why do you worry about the rest? Consider how the lilies grow. They do not labor or spin. Yet I tell you, not even Solomon in all his splendor was dressed like one of these. If that is how God clothes the grass of the field, which is here today, and tomorrow is thrown into the fire, how much more will he clothe you, O you of little faith! And do not set your heart on what you will eat or drink; do not worry about it. For the pagan world runs after all such things, and your Father knows that you need them. But seek his kingdom, and these things will be given to you as well. (Luke 12:22–31)

What about you? Are you letting your heart fill up with trouble and fear, or are you enjoying Father's promise of peace and provision?

Needless to say, I never went to work at Wal-Mart. That would have been like Jonah running to Tarshish instead of Nineveh! I thank the Lord that He gave me the strength to keep doing what I was called to do, and He always provided. If I had gone to work at Wal-Mart (Tarshish), I wouldn't be writing this book today—I'm convinced of it!

God Provides at the Speed of Suddenly

When God shows up, often He shows up suddenly. On the day of Pentecost, "*suddenly a sound like the blowing of a violent wind came from heaven and filled the whole house where they were sitting*" (Acts 2:2, emphasis added). When Paul was persecuting the Christians, "*suddenly a light from heaven flashed around him*" (Acts 9:3, emphasis added), and he fell to the ground in a great encounter with God. When Peter was in prison, "*Suddenly an angel of the Lord appeared*" (Acts 12:7, emphasis added), caused his chains to come off, and led him to freedom.

Today, God still moves at the speed of *suddenly*—when God's will and God's timing intersect, *suddenly* you receive your breakthrough; *suddenly* the promise of God is fulfilled after you have waited patiently. Therefore, we must always be expecting our *suddenlys* from the Lord. If we aren't expecting our *suddenlys*, we aren't ready when the *suddenlys* come. Our *suddenlys* are just up ahead, so we'd better get ready. We don't want to miss that business deal, ministry opportunity, or job opening we have been waiting for.

When God suddenly provides or acts on our behalf, He requires sudden action on our parts—immediate, total obedience to the leading of the Holy Spirit. If God suddenly says, "Give," we'd better give suddenly. If God suddenly says, "Pray," we'd better pray suddenly. If God suddenly says, "Go there and do this," we'd better go there and do what He says. As we take care of the sudden actions that God is requiring of us, He will take care of His sudden actions on our behalf.

Father knows the awesome plans He has for your life—"*plans to prosper you and not to harm you, plans to give you hope and a future*" (Jeremiah 29:11)—and He wants you to know His plans for you, as well. You can know when your *suddenly* is on the horizon if you maintain a life of prayer, which will enable you to hear God's voice and sense His direction. Then, when you are clued in on the plan, you can expect your *suddenly*—a *suddenly* filled with hope, prosperity, and a bright future.

Today, when I look back over my life, I can honestly say, "God is so good." Many of the storms that I have been through seem as though they were from another lifetime. *Suddenly* the sun was shining again. *Suddenly* a new day appeared on the horizon. *Suddenly* the pain dissipated from my heart. *Suddenly* the Son was shining through me with a new and glorious brightness. *Suddenly!*

More Lessons in Faith for Financial Provision

Trust God, Not Other People, for Provision

When we are in the midst of financial hardship, we have to be careful not to get angry and upset with those around us whom we *think* should be helping us. This is true for all of us—single moms, single dads, married couples, businesspeople, and those in ministry alike. We should always look to the Lord for our provision and not rely on the "arm of the flesh." (See, for example, 2 Chronicles 32:8.)

God had taught me this lesson long before I was a single mom, but for a time, I forgot this "faith lesson" in the face of mounting financial pressure. While traveling as a young evangelist, I would look around and think, "Okay, who's going to help me now?"

One day, after I became a single mom, I was staring at my file cabinet and considering all of the bills bulging out of the folder marked "Due," and I began to get angry. I thought, *My dad could write one check and pay every bill I have. He wouldn't even miss it! This would be a small amount for him.* Anger and resentment began to mount in my heart.

Then, the Lord said, "It's not his responsibility to pay your bills now that you are grown. But I'm your heavenly Father, and I can write one check and pay every bill you have. And I definitely wouldn't miss it, because I own it all."

I realized that God not only *could* pay my bills but also *would*—if I'd just trust Him. God has a way of getting right to the point with a word of truth. The truth was, I shouldn't have looked to my dad or anyone else for my provision. My heavenly Father was just waiting for me to look to Him. And today, your heavenly Father is waiting for you, too, to look to Him for your every need.

> YOUR HEAVENLY FATHER IS WAITING FOR YOU, TOO, TO LOOK TO HIM FOR YOUR EVERY NEED.

Provision Often Comes from Unlikely Places

Father will always get His provision into our hands, but the channel by which it comes is often the least expected or the seemingly unlikeliest. I'm convinced that the Lord *sets us up* to *build us up*. The setup is that the necessary funds almost never come from the expected source, and the buildup is for our faith. Father builds up our faith during every step of this marvelous journey we are on with Him.

Once, while holding my second citywide youth crusade, I owed a large amount to the convention center. I had already learned a few "faith lessons," but I still had quite a ways to go. Experience had taught me that if the provision I needed didn't come from the offering collected at the church where I was preaching, it could be waiting for me in my mailbox when I returned home. It had taken me a while to learn this faith lesson, however.

As I was preparing for the crusade, I knew that a lot of young people would be saved and ministered to. *But where in the world is the financial support going to come from?* I wondered. Many people had made commitments to give, but when the time had come to do so, they had backed out for various reasons. Just one day prior to the payment's due date, I was ministering in a small church a few hours away. As the service closed that Sunday morning, I still didn't have the needed funds that were due the following day. I felt the Lord leading me to drive to Oklahoma City that afternoon to attend a service that evening. I hadn't even been thinking about the needed funds because I hadn't been scheduled to minister in Oklahoma City, yet I felt very strongly that the Lord was saying I needed to be there. The young girl who was traveling with me at the time, Shea, drove the van, and we arrived in Oklahoma City just in time for the evening service.

Much to my surprise, the youth pastor who was leading the service began to talk about the upcoming youth crusade I was preparing for.

Someone in the congregation stopped him and said, "The young lady evangelist who's holding this event is here tonight." The youth pastor then asked me to come up to the platform and share about the crusade. I did, and as I concluded my remarks, he took the microphone and said, "This is a God thing, and if God tells you to help her in any way, please do."

At the close of the service, Shea and I went separate ways, talking to people and shaking hands. As the crowd dispersed, I was left standing alone—and without any financial gift. I found Shea, and as the two of us started to make our way outside to the van, she began telling me what had happened in the back of the church after the service.

She said, "Did you see that lady in the last row—the one who was in a wheelchair?"

I responded, "No."

Shea replied, "After the service, she motioned for me to come over to where she was, and she asked what we needed. I told her, 'Seven thousand dollars by tomorrow morning,' and she wrote me a check."

Talk about shouting for joy! We were both overwhelmed. As soon as our excitement died down, however, I began to think, *What if the check isn't any good?*

The next morning, we went straight to the bank. When we asked the teller to cash the check, she got a strange look on her face and asked us to take a seat in the waiting area for a minute. My mind began to go wild with doubts. I thought, *This is a bad check, and they think we are responsible. What if they are calling the police? What if this, and what if that?*

One minute felt like an eternity. When the teller finally called us back to the window, she apologized for any inconvenience and told us that she had just called the account holder to make sure she had, indeed, written the check. The teller informed us that everything was fine and then cashed the check.

The Lord taught me a valuable faith lesson that day—a lesson about looking to Him for provision. The last person I would have expected the funds to come from was a lady whom I didn't know in the back row at a church where I hadn't even been scheduled to speak.

Part two of that lesson was when God said, "You had enough faith to get that check into your hand, but you didn't have enough faith to believe that it was good."

God, You've Got Mail!

When Jesus was teaching His disciples to pray, He included the phrase, *"Give us today our daily bread"* (Matthew 6:11). He didn't say, "Give us today our monthly bread." He said *"our daily bread."* I don't know about you, but I kind of like to have the whole month budgeted out. And, if it's possible, I like to know my budget for the upcoming year!

But God doesn't usually work that way. His way requires us to walk by faith and trust Him. When He told me, "But I'm your heavenly Father, and I can write one check and pay every bill you have. And I definitely wouldn't miss it, because I own it all," He got through to me, loud and clear—so clear that I began to treat every incoming bill as if it didn't have my name on it.

Whenever I would find a pile of bills in my post office box, I'd simply look up and say, "God, You've got mail!" Then, I'd take God's bills home and put them in the folder labeled "Due." I wouldn't open that folder again until money was put in my hand. At that time, I'd say, "Okay, God, which of Your bills do You want me to pay for You?"

The Lord taught me to take comfort in the knowledge that everything I have comes from Him. Every dollar, every food item, every piece of clothing—everything comes from Him. He also taught me to ask Him what He wanted me to do with every dollar that came into my hand. That was an important key to having all of my needs met.

Philippians 4:19 says, *"My God will meet all your needs according to his glorious riches in Christ Jesus."* If my needs aren't met, then something is wrong. Maybe the *something* is that I spent God's money on something I wanted or thought I needed instead of paying one of His bills or giving to His church. As we learn to ask God what He wants us to do with every provision He puts in our hands, we can be free from stress and worry. We can say, "God, You've got mail!"

God Provides at His Appointed Place of Positioning

God wants to position us to prosper. His desire is for you and me to prosper spiritually, emotionally, physically, and financially. As we submit

GOD'S DESIRE IS FOR YOU AND ME TO PROSPER SPIRITUALLY, EMOTIONALLY, PHYSICALLY, AND FINANCIALLY.

to the positioning process of the Holy Spirit, we will step into our Father's abundant provision. In other words, we have to be where we are supposed to be, when we are supposed to be there, doing what we are supposed to be doing, and doing it for the right reasons. Because I obeyed the Lord by staying in Virginia Beach and continuing to do what I was called to do, the Lord's provision was always there—always!

If the Lord tells you to take a job with a salary that's half of what you are making now, you'd better obey. If the Lord tells you to move, but you want to stay where you are, you'd better move anyway. The key is obedience. As we submit to the will of the Father through the leading of the Holy Spirit, we will step into God's abundant provision. But if we resist the Father's leading and go our own ways, we will never have enough, because Father's provision is always at His place of positioning.

If you are willing and obedient, you will eat the best from the land.

(Isaiah 1:19)

The Word says *if*. In other words, it depends upon our choices. *If* we are willing and obedient, we will step into God's best for us. It's easy to be willing but harder to be obedient. Many times, I've prayed, "Lord, help me be willing to be obedient."

Watch and pray so that you will not fall into temptation. The spirit is willing, but the body is weak. (Matthew 26:41)

In other words, we have to carry our willingness all the way through to obedience. If our flesh submits to the Spirit, and we walk in obedience, we set ourselves up to receive God's blessings. Obedience always brings blessings.

When Joseph was hanging out in the pit, I'm sure it didn't look to him like he was positioned to prosper. It probably looked like a dead end. In reality, though, it was a direct route to the palace. After Joseph was thrown into the pit, he was sold into slavery. Still, he prospered because the Lord was with him. And the Lord was with him because Joseph was in the will of God. Joseph prospered with success and favor. When you have the favor of God, which comes when you're obedient to Him, you can't help but be successful. And when you have the favor of God, you can't help but have the favor of man. You might be in a position that looks like a dead end. Yet, like Joseph, you can find favor everywhere you go.

The pit is a heavily populated place, but please don't be one who stays put in the pit because of despair, doubt, and disobedience. Have faith, and get back on the path to the palace!

Chapter Ten: From the Pit of Doubt and Despair to the Peak of Trust and Hope

Points to Ponder

1. You must learn to doubt your doubts and face your fears. Why is this critical to your being able to fulfill God's purpose for your life?

2. When God shows up, He often does so suddenly. Can you remember a time when God showed up suddenly for you? If so, describe it.

3. When God suddenly acts on your behalf, He requires sudden action on your part. What form of action is He requiring of you today, and why?

4. Provision from God often comes from unlikely places. Why do you think this is true?

5. What lesson can be learned from Joseph's life with regard to God causing him to prosper?

Meditate on these Scriptures, speak them aloud, and commit them to memory.

"For I know the plans I have for you," declares the Lord, *"plans to prosper you and not to harm you, plans to give you hope and a future."*
(Jeremiah 29:11)

So do not fear, for I am with you; do not be dismayed, for I am your God. I will strengthen you and help you; I will uphold you with my righteous right hand. (Isaiah 41:10)

He who dwells in the secret place of the Most High shall abide under the shadow of the Almighty. (Psalm 91:1 NKJV)

You will keep in perfect peace him whose mind is steadfast, because he trusts in you. (Isaiah 26:3)

—11—

FROM THE PIT OF LACK TO THE PEAK OF PLENTY

One day, when Destiny was about nine months old, the Lord told me to go to Tampa, Florida, to see some pastors I knew there. *Go to Florida?* I thought in disbelief. *I've had to believe God for gas money just to get around town, and He's saying, 'Go to Florida'?* I had peace in my spirit about it, but I had only one-sixteenth of a tank of gas. Nevertheless, I allowed peace to rule in the decision, and I made plans to take a trip to Tampa as if I had all the money I needed in the bank.

I made arrangements for a friend to travel with me to help with Destiny, but I didn't announce to anyone the financial need I had. Actually, I told only a couple of people about the trip. I set the date, and as our departure day approached, I didn't have five cents. What I *did* have was that big file folder labeled "Due" filled with God's bills, which would still be there when I returned.

Everything was set. The pastors in Tampa knew I was coming. The day before we were to leave for Florida, a dear friend of mine, Eve, had a yard sale, and I went to her house to help out. She was excited as she shared with me her plans for the day's proceeds. She had a successful sale, and I rejoiced with her, never mentioning my need. She didn't know that I was leaving for Tampa the next morning.

After a long, hot day in the sun at the yard sale, Destiny and I returned home to prepare for our trip, still not knowing how in the world we would get to Tampa the following day. When I was packing our bags and loading our van, someone knocked on my door. It was the woman from church who would often give me diapers. She'd showed up unexpectedly with two bags of diapers *and* thirty jars of baby food—exactly what I would need for the ten-day trip to Tampa. Talk about rejoicing! God had come through once again, and I hadn't even told the diaper woman I was in need. She had never given me baby food before, but she said, "God put it on my heart to bring these to you today." Well, she'd heard God, all right, and we rejoiced together as I shared that Destiny and I were leaving the next morning for a trip.

My faith took a huge leap as this woman left my home; I felt so "high" in the Lord that I could have run to Tampa if I'd needed to. I continued to rejoice in the Lord as I prepared for bed. The hours passed quickly, and before I knew it, the clock read 11:00 p.m. Not long after that, I heard another knock at my door. *Who in the world could be at my door this time of night?* I thought. I peeked out from behind the curtain and saw Eve standing on my porch.

I quickly opened the door and asked, "Is everything all right?"

Her smile erased my concern, and she asked to come in. Moments later, to my surprise, she pulled a large Ziploc baggie out of her purse and said, "As I was counting all of my yard sale money tonight, the Lord told me I was supposed to give it all to you."

I quickly reminded her of her own needs, which we had discussed earlier that day, yet she said, "I must obey the Lord."

Eve went on to tell me exactly how much money was in the baggie—to the very penny. I had calculated earlier how much I would need in gas money, and what she said was the exact amount. I then shared with her how her obedience to God was enabling me to walk in obedience—she hadn't known that I was leaving for Tampa the next morning.

God's illogical instructions never have to make sense to our natural minds. We must only walk in obedience to do what the Father says. Remember, money is never a problem to the Lord, so don't let money be a problem for you—Daddy owns it all!

While I was in Florida, the Lord moved the hearts of several ministers to bless me financially, even when I had not shared anything about my financial need with them. I returned to Virginia Beach with more than enough money to pay my mortgage that month—hallelujah!

The Great Setup

The more time I spent with the Lord, the more illogical instructions I got—illogical to my natural mind, that is. As I was driving home from Tampa, the Lord spoke to me again. This time, He revealed to me how to raise the funds I needed for Joy Ministries. We had recently been offered local airtime to begin a television ministry. I had waited thirteen years to do this, but it still didn't seem like the right time to begin. I thought, *I'm having to believe God for diapers and baby food, and now we are starting the television ministry?* But God's timing is not our timing. I'm convinced that He does things the way He does so He will get all the glory.

> I'M CONVINCED THAT GOD DOES THINGS THE WAY HE DOES SO HE WILL GET ALL THE GLORY.

These instructions would be another example of what I call the great setup. God sets us up so that we can grow in our faith and strengthen our trust in Him. When He does things, His ways and His timing are such that we couldn't try to take the credit, even if we wanted to. It was very obvious to me, and to everyone around me, that it was God who opened the door for my television ministry to begin. Several local ministries had offered to let me use their television equipment and even their church buildings to begin recording my television program. But, when it came down to it, everyone changed his or her mind, and some wouldn't even return my calls.

As I was beginning to feel discouraged, the Lord said clearly to me, "Just use what you have."

I thought, *Use what I have? I have my house and I have my car.*

He responded, "That's right—use your house."

So, that's just what I did.

I decided to record our television program in the living room of my townhouse. I knew that royal blue was a good background color for TV, but that was the extent of my knowledge about TV ministry. I could teach and preach—I had done those for years—but TV was a whole new experience for me. With my limited knowledge, I scraped together enough change to purchase what would be my first backdrop—a royal blue sheet from Bed, Bath & Beyond. When I finally found the color that I needed, I was shocked at the price—it was over $36. *Wow*, I thought, *that's a lot. I'm going to have to fast this week and use my grocery money to purchase the sheet.*

During my week of fasting, I opened my brand-new, royal blue sheet set, only to find that it had creases all over it from the packaging. This meant that I needed to get my new backdrop pressed at the local dry cleaner because ironing it wasn't effective. That was another unexpected expense, and—you guessed it—I fasted a little bit longer.

God was teaching me to listen to His voice. While in Tampa, I had mentioned to my pastor friends that I knew where I was going—I knew what God had called me to do. But now, under the circumstances, I had no idea how I was going to get there. In the months following my trip to Tampa, the Lord revealed a great spiritual truth to me that I will never forget: We get to where we are going one step of obedience at a time.

As I listened to the Lord and took a step of obedience each day to do what He was telling me to do, the call of God on my life continued to unfold. We must never despise small beginnings. (See Zechariah 4:10.) If we despise small beginnings, it's because we have pride hidden in our hearts. Many people were saved and encouraged by watching on TV as I preached under the anointing of the Holy Spirit in my living room. With the blue sheet behind me and a rented pulpit in front of me, I spoke, and lives were changed.

As I continued to take steps of obedience, the Lord's provision continued to flow. We should make our decisions according to the leading of the Holy Spirit, not according to the leading of our bank accounts. Let me share with you just a few more of my many stories so you'll be further encouraged never to make a decision based on a lack of finances.

Sowing a Seed I'd Reserved for My Own Need

It was about the fifth of the month, and my ex-husband had just given me a check for $100 for that month (child support had not yet been set). The night after he gave me the check, I had a dream in which the Lord told me to send $100 to a pastor's daughter whom I knew in Delaware. As I awoke from the dream and sat up in bed, I thought to myself, *That couldn't have been God—I don't have $100.*

I started to lie back down, and before my head hit the pillow, the Lord said, "Yes, you do. You were just given a $100 check today."

He'd jarred my memory, and I hastily responded, "But that's all I have for the rest of the month."

Have you ever noticed that we always give God information He already knows? He gave me a choice that night to walk in obedience or to walk in disobedience. The truth was, $100 wasn't enough for us to live on for the month, anyway. I immediately pulled myself up out of bed and went downstairs to write a check for $100, then put it in an envelope and sealed it before I could talk myself out of walking in obedience. The next morning, after I had woken up Destiny, the first thing I did was take the stamped envelope to the post office. As I dropped it in the mailbox, I prayed over my "seed."

Not only did Father provide for Destiny and me that month, but we also had enough money coming in through Joy Ministries to fund a mission trip to Bolivia. It was Destiny's first mission trip, and God used us both greatly in the lives of those precious people. You know, it takes a lot more to get to Bolivia than to Tampa! The Lord was challenging me to exercise my faith, and my seed brought in the needed harvest.

We must sow where and when Father tells us to sow, for then, we will reap a harvest from our seed. The truth is, I wanted to keep my $100; if I had been planning to sow it, I would have chosen another place. An important key is not waiting until we have enough to sow. Rather, we sow when Father tells us to sow. The second key is knowing where the Lord wants us to sow. To figure that out, we must be walking in obedience.

A woman who watched our TV program wanted to attend our annual women's conference but figured she wouldn't be able to go, since she was out of a job and could not really afford the registration fee of $39. However, in her heart, she saw the conference as an opportunity to sow. Believing God for a miracle, she sowed the registration fee. She attended the conference on Saturday, and on Monday, she received a phone call from a company where she had applied and was asked to report for work on Tuesday. What a great reward for obeying God's guidance and sowing her need!

A Tempting Fix for Cold Showers

When you are in the mission field, you expect to go without the comforts of home. You know that it's temporary, and that, in a few weeks, you'll return to your beloved amenities. But what about when your comfort zone is messed with at home?

One day, I was taking a shower, and the water didn't get very warm, even though it had been running for quite some time. I rushed through my shower routine and hopped out, reaching for my towel. I thought it was strange, but I was quickly distracted by the cry demanding Mommy's presence in another room. A little while later, I was washing the dishes and noticed that the water was still cold.

I called a repairman, hopeful that my hot water would be restored quickly. After examining the unit, however, he announced that I would need a whole new water heater. The good news was that he did that kind of work, so he could definitely fix the problem. The bad news was that it was going to cost me $530. I immediately told him that I didn't have even $5. He went on to tell me that he accepted credit cards. Yet the Lord clearly told me not to put anything on my credit card, reminding me that He, not my Visa card, was my Provider.

I must say, it was very tempting to rely on my Visa card—I had been heating Destiny's bathwater on the stove and had already gone a few days without a hot or even warm shower—and the temptation would become even greater in the days ahead. But I thanked the repairman and assured him that he would be hearing from me as soon as the Lord put the money in my hand.

Day after day, I would heat water on the stove to bathe Destiny and give myself little sponge baths in the sink. Believe me, this got old really quick! I kept quoting Scriptures like Philippians 4:19: *"My God shall supply all* [my] *need according to His riches in glory"* (NKJV). My faith would rise up within me as I spoke the Word, but it would shrink back again as I allowed thoughts and doubts from my natural mind to kick in.

One day, while I was washing clothes and dishes in cold water, the phone rang. It was a pharmaceutical company that had come across an old résumé of mine that I had distributed; because of my experience in hotel sales and retail, they figured I would make an excellent salesperson. They were looking for a sales representative for my area, and they wanted to know if I was interested. Before I had a chance to answer, they informed me that the base salary was $65,000 a year, plus commission. The position also included a cell phone and a car allowance. Immediately, I had visions of hot showers, no more heating water in pans on the stove, and a much-needed car payment supplied for me. I thought, *It must be God—right?*

As tempting as the offer was, the Holy Spirit kept saying, "Just keep doing what you're called to do. Just keep on keeping on."

As hard as it was, I turned down the tempting offer. I thought to myself, *I must be crazy. My brain has frozen from all of the cold water, and now I'm not even thinking rationally.* I was right—it seemed irrational and illogical to turn down the offer, and the fact that I had done so didn't make any sense to my natural mind.

I began to analyze the timing of the offer. How unusual it was for a company to call me out of the clear blue! On top of that, the offer had come at a very low point—I had no hot water with which to wash my daughter. The enemy tries really hard to get us to fall for his detours by introducing them when we're most vulnerable. Remember—don't even flirt with a detour. Stay focused on the instructions the Lord has given you.

Days passed, and even though I had hoped that the water in my house would miraculously get warmer on its own, it didn't. I tried laying hands on my water heater and commanding it to work, in the name of Jesus—after all, I had resurrected my broken-down, beat-up car that way several times. Hey, there's power in prayer, so I thought I'd go for it.

One day, weeks after my water heater had stopped working, I received a call from my older brother. I knew something was up because he doesn't call often. After reassuring me that everyone back home was all right, he mentioned that while cleaning out his closets, he'd found some old savings bonds that my grandmother had given me years before. While I'd been away at college, I had asked him to keep them for me. He had tucked them away in a safe place but then hadn't been able to remember where that safe place was for many years. He went on to inform me that the total value of the bonds would be around $500, and he was just wondering if I wanted him to mail them to me or continue saving them for me. I tried to be calm, cool, and collected in my response, because I had not communicated to my family the difficult financial situation that I was in.

I responded, "Oh, go ahead and mail them." With uncontrollable excitement, I quickly added, "Could you put them in the mail today?"

He promptly forwarded me my savings bonds, and I all but camped out at the post office. Two days later, I received the much-anticipated envelope and went straight to the bank. Within minutes, I walked out with $535 in cash in my hand. I called the repairman to schedule the installation of a new water heater, informing him that I now had $530 to pay for it. Moments later, I went through the drive thru at Chick-fil-A and treated myself to my favorite salad with the leftover $5. Wow! God had come through again!

Not only did I receive the needed funds for my hot water heater, but now, I was also stepping into the abundant provision of God—I had five bucks more than I needed! I thought, *This is the life—a salad at Chick-fil-A.* Don't laugh; you'd think so too if you fasted as much as I did.

Corn Dogs Galore

Buying food was a challenge for quite a while. I had to pay all God's bills first, and then I'd buy groceries if there was anything left. One evening, during a special service at church, the guest evangelist asked that everyone in attendance give $25 in the offering. Anyone who did not have $25 was to raise a hand so that the evangelist could give $25 for that person. I immediately felt embarrassed, but then recognized that feeling as pride. Swallowing my pride, I raised my hand.

After the ushers passed the offering plates, the Lord spoke to me: "You said you didn't have it." He was referring to the $26 in my checkbook. I went on to explain silently to the Lord that the $26 was my grocery money, and that it was all I had for the rest of the month.

He responded, "But you said you didn't *have* it." I got the point and rushed out of my seat to catch the ushers, who were already preparing to exit at the back of the sanctuary. As I sowed the $25 seed, I prayed that there were no errors in my checkbook. If I had miscalculated, the check probably would have bounced. A bounced check would cost me about three weeks' worth of grocery money—not good!

Once again, I started a fast. It's easy to feel "led" to fast when you don't have any food in the house. About four or five days later, I received a phone call from a lady I knew. She said, "Danette, I was just wondering if you had any need for food."

Trying once again to remain calm, I replied, "Sure, I guess I could use some."

She went on to tell me that a local grocery store was giving her frozen meats and other food items that had passed their expiration dates but were still safe to eat. She went on to say that she had an abundant supply that she would receive twice every month.

I said, "I'll be right over."

I had never really liked corn dogs, but after you fast for a couple of weeks, they taste like filet mignon. We had so many corn dogs that our freezer couldn't store them all. Twice a month for almost two years, this lady would also give me large trash bags filled with lunchmeat of all kinds mixed in with other food items.

Whenever Destiny and I would get sick of corn dogs and begin to complain about the "manna" the Lord had provided, He would direct me to fast. Our gratitude for God's provision would always return after about twenty-four hours of fasting, at which point the thought of eating corn dogs would suddenly become appealing again.

The abundance of frozen meat we received became the beginning of our food ministry to the poor and needy in our community. On a regular basis, Destiny and I would take food to the single moms and their children living in local subsidized housing areas. This entire ministry started with a $25 seed sown in obedience. With $25 of what was supposed to be my budgeted grocery money, the Lord fed us and multiple other families for more than two years. To this day, we are not eager to eat corn dogs, but we definitely have grateful hearts for God's provision in all its forms, including corn dogs.

The God of the Wind and the Rain

Due to its position on the East Coast, Virginia Beach has always had more than its fair share of tropical storms and hurricanes. Destiny was probably about two years old when a hurricane came through and took off half of our roof. My first thought after assessing the damage was, *Now I not only have to pay the mortgage, but I also have to pay for a new roof.*

A few days later, as the shock of this new devastation wore off, I was reminded to call my insurance company. I was praying that they would give me enough to replace the roof, and also that the monthly premium would not increase on my homeowner's policy.

It took several weeks for an adjuster to come to our home because thousands of other homeowners were in the same situation as we. When the adjuster finally arrived, he first assessed the roof damage, then came inside to check out any interior damage to our home. I took him upstairs to view the water stains on the ceiling in three different rooms. The water stains were about the size of an orange, yet he took out his measuring tape and recorded the perimeter of each room. In the bathroom, the wallpaper next to the water spot was peeling slightly, and this, too, was recorded in his report.

As he continued to calculate the measurements, he said, "Ma'am, we are going to pay for you to completely paint each of these rooms and for you to re-wallpaper this bathroom."

I immediately responded, "Oh, sir, I'm going to replace the roof, but I'm not going to repaint all of these rooms. And I'm just going to slap some glue on the back of that wallpaper and stick it back up there."

Remember, we were used to living extremely frugally, rationing toilet paper and eating corn dogs night after night. The thought of spending money to replace all of the wallpaper didn't seem even close to practical.

The man expressed appreciation for my honesty but went on to say, "Ma'am, this is why you have homeowner's insurance, and our policy requires us to pay for the total replacement of this wallpaper and for the painting of all of these rooms. What you do or don't do with the money is up to you, but I'm required to pay you for all of these items on my list."

Well, hey, who was I to argue with a man who wanted to give me money? I wanted to be totally honest, because I knew that without honesty, I couldn't expect the blessing and favor of God to be on me.

> GOD SAID, "I'M THE GOD OF THE WIND AND THE RAIN. I CAN DO WHATEVER I WANT TO DO TO GET MY PROVISION TO YOU."

Within days, I received a check large enough to pay for my roof to be replaced and to pay my mortgage that month. I rejoiced, I shouted, and I once again repented of my former threats to secure a job at Wal-Mart.

As I opened the check and saw the blessing of the Lord, He said, "I'm the God of the wind and the rain. I can do whatever I want to do to get My provision to you."

I not only received a new roof, which I'd needed even before the storm, but God once again paid His bill on time, too.

God's Faithfulness Sees Us through Setbacks

Each day, I would take steps to go forward in fulfilling the call of God on my life. God was blessing our TV ministry, and we received more and more airtime—for free! People were getting saved and being blessed by the teachings and encouragement coming into their living rooms each night.

Destiny and I were also taking steps to go forward in our life as a family. It had been more than four years since my husband and I had separated and two years since our divorce had been finalized. The Lord had been teaching me that a healthy, stable, godly home was what my daughter needed. Although I was a single parent, the Lord encouraged me that He and I together could give Destiny the home that she needed.

Just as things seemed to be getting settled in our lives, we received some devastating news. One night, around eleven o'clock, I received a phone call informing me that my former husband was dead. *How can that be?* I thought. *I just ran into him a few weeks ago.* Destiny was fast asleep when I received the call, and I was glad for that. She was four years old and had preschool in the morning. I quickly called a couple of my close friends, who immediately came over and spent the night with me.

The days and months that followed were very difficult. I wasn't given any clear details concerning the circumstances that surrounded his death, which made it even worse. I was the ex-wife, so getting any kind of information was more than difficult.

Just two years prior, on my birthday—January 16, 2001—my divorce had been made final. On January 16, 2003, I was sitting at the funeral service of my former husband. It was a difficult time for all of us, and the death was much harder to deal with than the divorce. Death is so final—there's no hope for any type of restoration of relationship; there's no way to turn the clock back.

Several months later, another single mother approached me and said, "You've got it easy. I still have to deal with my ex-husband, and you don't."

That comment grieved me in my spirit, and I quickly responded, "Don't ever say or think that again. Death is very difficult, and your children still have their father alive."

Several days later, the mother apologized for her comment. I encouraged her again to be grateful that her children still had a father who was alive. There's only one pain greater to a child than the pain of divorce, and that's the pain of death. The amount of trauma and anguish sustained by a child due to the death of a parent is tremendous, and only the Lord can bring comfort and relief. As the psalmist said, *"A father to the fatherless, a defender of widows, is God in his holy dwelling"* (Psalm 68:5).

As we were dealing with all of the emotions surrounding my ex-husband's death, I received notice that Destiny's health insurance would automatically be cancelled at the end of the month because she had been on her father's policy. Also, child support would no longer be put toward my account. After reviewing our divorce papers, I made a phone call to my ex-husband's former employer to request the benefits due to Destiny as the beneficiary of his life insurance policy. The gentleman on the other end of the line reluctantly informed me that her name was not on the policy.

He researched other possible benefits that children of the company's deceased employees could qualify for, but then said with regret in his voice, "We've never had anyone fall through every crack like you, Ms. Crawford. I'm sorry."

He informed me that Destiny's father had opted out of participation in Social Security during his entire career with them. This choice is available for only a few occupations. But he encouraged me to contact the Social Security office, anyway. The Social Security employee said, "Lady, we can't pay out what was never paid in." So, I received only a small trickle of the money he had deposited from jobs held during his teenage years.

God was still in control. Even though we had fallen through every crack with my ex-husband's former employer, we never fell though any crack with the Lord. God was again setting us up to be totally dependent on Him. Around the end of the month—see the pattern?—I received a phone call from someone asking what we needed.

I quickly responded, "I need health insurance for Destiny. Her policy will be cancelled within days."

The caller said, "Don't worry; we'll pay for her insurance." I hung up the phone feeling very relieved.

The next day, the phone rang again. It was the same person, but, this time, she had a different question. She asked, "How much do you owe on your home?"

I retrieved the proper document and answered her question down to the penny. She said, "I'll tell you what. We're not going to pay for Destiny's insurance." My mouth temporarily dropped open, only to form a huge smile when she added, "But, we are going to pay off your house for you."

God is so good. In the time of my greatest need, He brought me the greatest blessing. I had $7.80 in my checkbook. Within days, I received the promised cashier's check. I deposited the cashier's check and wrote out my own check to the mortgage company. After this check cleared, my balance was once again $7.80—but my house had been paid off. Glory to God! We had a corn dog celebration that night, and I kissed the thought of a job at Wal-Mart good-bye, once and for all!

> GOD IS SO GOOD. IN THE TIME OF MY GREATEST NEED, HE BROUGHT ME THE GREATEST BLESSING.

Chapter Eleven: From the Pit of Lack to the Peak of Plenty

Points to Ponder

1. Has God ever given you an illogical instruction? What was it, and what was the result of your obeying it?

2. Why do you think God gives us instructions that just don't make any sense to our natural minds?

3. God wants you to listen to all of His instructions, and He'll often give you illogical ones. What must you allow the Holy Spirit to do for you during times like these?

4. When you are faced with challenging circumstances in life, what is the best thing for you to remember?

5. I have shared many of my personal "faith lessons" with you in this chapter. Think back over your life and write down several faith lessons that you have learned in your hard places.

Meditate on these Scriptures, speak them aloud, and commit them to memory.

Teach me to do your will, for you are my God; may your good Spirit lead me on level ground. (Psalm 143:10)

And my God will meet all your needs according to his glorious riches in Christ Jesus. (Philippians 4:19)

If you are willing and obedient, you will eat the best from the land. (Isaiah 1:19)

Give, and it will be given to you. A good measure, pressed down, shaken together and running over, will be poured into your lap. (Luke 6:38)

—12—

FROM THE PIT OF WHINING TO THE PEAK OF WINNING

During my first few years as a single mom, I faced the temptation to whine like never before. I experienced so many different emotions every day, and my sense of rejection was at an all-time high. The rejection I'd felt from my father when I was growing up came rushing back with even greater intensity as I faced my own divorce. I felt like such a failure. Although it was my marriage that had failed, I felt as though *I* had failed.

The hormonal changes that result from having a baby are usually enough to make any woman whine. These changes were combined with a nightly lack of sleep I experienced from caring for my baby daughter that lasted at least nine months. I can remember sitting on the floor and crying in the middle of the night because I was so tired and emotionally broken (not to mention financially broke). Once again, I experienced the kind of anger I'd felt for years toward my father for leaving me—this time directed toward my husband. I was angry to have been left with all of the responsibilities.

Whining appeared to be my only option. After all, I deserved to whine—no one had it as hard as me, right? I wanted to start a Whiners Club, complete with monthly newsletters and daily conference calls. I can't tell you how many times I was tempted to recruit members. But, out of His goodness, God kept my club's enrollment to a minimum!

The Lord taught me a lot about the lifestyles and choices of whiners versus winners. At every step during the years He was teaching me, I had to make a choice to think, act, and talk like a winner, not a whiner. Daily,

I had to choose to allow the Holy Spirit to raise up the winner within me. Daily, I had to choose not to give voice to the whiner in me but rather to proclaim the Word of the Lord over my daughter and myself.

Every time I pressed forward and refused to be a whiner, the Holy Spirit would be right there with the Father's grace and mercy for each day, enabling me to move forward one step of obedience at a time.

Whiners always talk about what they are going through, but winners always talk about where they are going to—the finish line. If we are honest, we'll admit that there is a little "whiner" in all of us. But we must make that whiner submit to the Spirit of the Lord within us.

Whiners versus Winners

What are the differences between whiners and winners? Let's look at their opposing characteristics together.

Whiners Hate Waiting;
Winners Respect God's Timing with Patience

Whiners hate to wait; they have no patience for it. They hate to wait in line, so they complain. They hate to wait in traffic and are usually the ones who exhibit road rage. They want things when they want them, how they want them. They don't even like to wait on God. If they have to wait on God and all of His promises, they start whining! They always want immediate gratification, and if they don't get it, they gripe.

> Yet the LORD longs to be gracious to you; he rises to show you compassion. For the LORD is a God of justice. Blessed are all who wait for him! (Isaiah 30:18)

Waiting is a part of life—a big, important part of life. And waiting on the Lord is at the top of the list. Psalm 27:14 says, "Wait for the LORD; be strong and take heart and wait for the LORD." Respecting God's timing is so important in every area of our lives. The very life of the butterfly depends on waiting for the caterpillar's transformation process to be completed.

Timing really is everything when it comes to the Lord, and those who wait on Him are truly blessed.

But when the time had fully come, God sent his Son, born of a woman, born under law, to redeem those under law, that we might receive the full rights of sons. (Galatians 4:4–5)

God doesn't do anything until the time has "*fully come.*" We can kick, we can scream, we can feel sorry for ourselves, but Father doesn't do anything until the proper time has fully come. When the time had fully come, God sent His Son—and not a moment before. When the time has fully come, we will see His promises fulfilled in our lives—not a moment earlier, and not a moment later.

Again, whiners don't like to wait for anything, but winners understand the importance of respecting God's timing. Because of this, they wait patiently. Like the psalmist, they can say, "*I waited patiently for the LORD; he turned to me and heard my cry*" (Psalm 40:1).

> WITH GOD, IT'S ALWAYS WORTH THE WAIT! HE HEARS OUR CRIES AND ANSWERS OUR PRAYERS—IN HIS TIMING.

Winners understand that they'll spend a lot of time in the "waiting room," but with God, it's always worth the wait! He hears our cries and answers our prayers—in His timing.

Whiners Stay in Their Comfort Zones; Winners Pursue Their Potential Zones

We have a comfort zone in every area of our lives—in our finances, our climates, our surroundings, our wills, our emotions, our minds, our relationships, and so forth. Whiners never want to get out of their comfort zones, and if they happen to do so, they immediately start whining! Winners, on the other hand, always accept the challenge to press past their comfort zones. They know that an important key to entering their potential zones is continually choosing to get out of their comfort zones.

In my ministry, everyone who goes through the volunteer training is asked in which area he or she would prefer to serve. Many respond, "Oh, anywhere you need me." But when we let them know they are needed in the nursery during one of our special events, for example, they often respond, "Well, anywhere but there." In other words, their comfort zones are being messed with, and they don't like it!

Winners don't deny the fact that their comfort zones are being messed with, yet they stay focused on their potential zones. They don't mind paying the price, because they are focused on the result—where they are going. They know they will never come into their potential zones if they don't press past their comfort zones.

Even Jesus had to press past His comfort zone in order to come into His potential zone. In the garden of Gethsemane, just before He was to be arrested and crucified, He prayed in desperation to the Father. *"Going a little farther, he fell with his face to the ground and prayed, 'My Father, if it is possible, may this cup be taken from me. Yet not as I will, but as you will'"* (Matthew 26:39).

Jesus said, in other words, "What You are asking me to do is really out of My comfort zone, but if You are requiring it of Me to come into My potential zone and My purpose, I will yield to Your will!"

Whiners Ask, "What If?"; Winners Ask, "Why Not?"

Whiners always want to play it safe. They are filled with fears and what-ifs: "What if I can't make it?" "What if I fail?" "What if I get rejected?" "What if I make a fool out of myself?" Fear paralyzes whiners and keeps them from stepping into what God has for them. They lean on man and put their trust in the flesh instead of in God, ignoring the Bible's caution: *"This is what the LORD says: 'Cursed is the one who trusts in man, who depends on flesh for his strength and whose heart turns away from the LORD'"* (Jeremiah 17:5).

Winners, on the other hand, say, "What if I miss this window of opportunity?" Winners trust God and go for it! Jeremiah 17:7 says, *"Blessed is the man who trusts in the LORD, whose confidence is in him."* Winners are blessed because they always trust God. Their confidence is in the Lord, not in themselves or other people. Winners are the first ones to get out of the boat, and they are willing to walk on water. They are wise in their choices and don't make rash decisions, yet they get out of the boat when God says it's time. (See Matthew 14:25–29.) Whiners need five hundred confirmations when they receive direction from God, and they still think it was just a coincidence!

In the book of Matthew, we see that when we don't recognize the Lord in our lives, we can become trapped and stalled by fear.

During the fourth watch of the night Jesus went out to them, walking on the lake. When the disciples saw him walking on the lake, they were terrified. "It's a ghost," they said, and cried out in fear. But Jesus immediately said to them: "Take courage! It is I. Don't be afraid."
(Matthew 14:25–27)

Winners can recognize the Lord, and they can hear those words— *"It is I. Don't be afraid"*—and then rest in God. Whiners are unable—or unwilling—to get past the element of fear. Most whiners have a root of fear operating in their lives. Fear is the opposite of faith. Fear listens to the voice of the enemy, while faith listens to the voice of God.

Whiners Speak the Negative; Winners Proclaim the Positive

Whiners always speak the word of their flesh. They say, "I can't do this. Life's not fair. I can't take it anymore."

While whiners always say why they can't do something, winners always say why they *can!* Winners speak the Word of the Lord; they give voice to the Spirit. Winners say, "God's grace is sufficient for me." (See 2 Corinthians 12:9.) They proclaim Philippians 4:13: *"I can do everything through him who gives me strength."*

Whiners Are Miserable; Winners Have More Fun

Whiners spend most of their time upset about something. Some of them actually get their identities from their problems or crises. They live with a victim mentality rather than a victor mentality. Winners, on the other hand, spend most of their time happy. They get excited about where they are going, and they celebrate even before they get there!

Whiners See What Is; Winners See What May Be

Whiners have few goals, if any. They are so busy whining, they don't have time to set goals. Besides, even if they have goals, they don't ever plan on reaching them because of their long lists of reasons why they can't.

Winners, on the other hand, are goal-oriented people with objectives for today, this week, this month, and this year. They also have long-term goals. Winners read the Word of God daily because they stand on the promises of God and rely on the Holy Spirit 100 percent. Winners know that they can't, but God can!

Whiners Attract Whiners; Winners Attract Winners

Whiners attract whiners, and winners attract winners. Whiners don't like to be around winners because winners won't whine along with them; they won't come to their pity parties. Winners speak the positive, and it drives whiners crazy.

Winners don't like to be around whiners, either. Whiners are always complaining, always talking negatively, and always saying why they can't do something. They talk constantly about what they are going through, rather than acknowledge that God will see them through it. Whiners and winners mix like oil and water—they don't. So, in relationships, their contrasting outlooks pose a problem.

I have learned that true friends don't come to your pity parties. True friends encourage you to "grow" forward. Actually, the devil is the only one who really likes attending our pity parties.

Whiners Are Derailed by Disappointments; Winners Revise Their Strategies and Move On

Whiners get stuck easily by failures and disappointments, but winners get reappointed quickly after each disappointment.

Hope deferred makes the heart sick, but a longing fulfilled is a tree of life. (Proverbs 13:12)

Yes, hope deferred—disappointment—makes our hearts sick. It's normal to grieve a loss or a plan that fails, but then we have to dry our tears and move on. We must focus on the second part of that verse—*"A longing fulfilled is a tree of life."* There are many longings that have been fulfilled in our lives, sprouting many trees of life. And we will have many longings fulfilled in the years to come. Winners are those who focus forward and maintain an attitude of gratitude. They don't focus on what they don't have; they focus on what they *do* have.

A whiner allows failure to become his identity and his destiny, but a winner understands what failure *is* and what it *isn't*. Failure is an opportunity to learn; it isn't who you are. Failure can also be not doing what God has told you to do—disobeying Him. But whenever we do what the Father tells us to do, we will be successful. Winners meet with success because they seek God's will and fulfill it obediently.

Success Is Found in Obeying God

I can remember my first few citywide crusades. I was in my mid-twenties, and I still had a lot to learn. I rented a big convention center in downtown Oklahoma City, and I thought people would just flock to the meeting. When they didn't, I felt like a failure. Even though we had over one thousand people in attendance during the course of the weekend, I felt like a failure.

The Lord asked me, "Did you do what I told you to do?"

I said, "Yes, Lord."

"Then, you were successful. Success is doing what I told you to do."

The Lord went on to explain by His Holy Spirit that if I took the responsibility on myself for having a small crowd, I would later take the glory for having a large crowd. The size of the crowd wasn't important; it was the size of my obedience that meant everything to the Lord. (See Judges 7, re; Gideon.)

Years later, when I got a divorce, I felt like a failure again. I had done everything I could possibly do, yet my marriage ended in a divorce. I had stood in faith for the restoration of my marriage; I had fasted and prayed for my husband's deliverance—yet my hopes were deferred, and my heart was sick! I had to press past the feelings of failure. I had walked in obedience to the Lord every step of the way, so I really had no reason to feel like a failure. Yes, my marriage had failed, but I wasn't a failure.

I focused instead on the longing that had been fulfilled in my life by the birth of my daughter. For years, I had wanted a little girl with long, blonde hair and big, blue eyes, and that's just what the Lord gave me. Though hope deferred makes the heart sick, all the longings fulfilled in our lives are trees of life.

The Father wants to raise up the winner in me, and then He wants to raise up the winner in all those with whom I come into contact. Again, whereas whiners always talk about what they are going through, winners always talk about where they are going to—the finish line. To whom am I giving voice today—the whiner or the winner? How about you?

Silencing the Whiner Within

It takes total surrender to the Lord in order for us to silence the "whiner" within. As we surrender the carnal things that we think, want, and feel to the Holy Spirit, we can experience all that Father has for us.

Dwell in the Secret Place of the Most High

During a storm, we run for cover. We go inside and take shelter from the elements. When we experience emotional and spiritual storms in our lives that tempt us to whine, we must do the same thing—run for cover in the secret place of the Most High. Psalm 91:1 says, *"He who dwells in the secret place of the Most High shall abide under the shadow of the Almighty"* (NKJV). As we dwell in the secret place of the Most High—through prayer, worship, reading His Word, and surrendering to His will—we can experience the Person and the power of the Holy Spirit.

Our wills are surrendered to whatever we want most. We may want to lose ten pounds, but if our desire for a piece of chocolate cake is greater than our desire to lose weight, we will probably surrender our wills to a chocolate fix instead of a smaller pant size. We may want to stop whining, but if the thing we're whining about out of disappointment is more important than our contentment in Christ, we'll keep on complaining.

When we desire the Lord and His presence more than anything else, we will surrender our lives to Him—our schedules, our activities, our priorities, our complaints—and spending time with our heavenly Father will be our number one priority.

Work with the Holy Spirit

The Holy Spirit is a Person, and He wants to fellowship with us all day, every day. I've said before that I believe in godly, professional counseling, but the greatest Counselor is the Holy Spirit. (See, for example, John 14:26.) The Holy Spirit leads us and guides us into all truth. (See John 16:13.) He will tell you all kinds of things that you could never know without spending time listening to His voice—things that will equip you to be a winner.

GOD WILL TELL YOU ALL KINDS OF THINGS THAT YOU COULD NEVER KNOW WITHOUT SPENDING TIME LISTENING TO HIS VOICE—THINGS THAT WILL EQUIP YOU TO BE A WINNER.

Matthew 11:15 says, *"He who has ears to hear, let him be listening and let him consider and perceive and comprehend by hearing"* (AMP). If we have ears to hear—if we listen to Him—the Lord will teach us all things. As parents, and especially if we're single parents, we need to listen to the wisdom of God to raise our children.

Whenever I had to go to court regarding child support, the Holy Spirit would be my Lawyer. The Lord would tell me what to say and what not to say. He would show me where to go to get information, and He would let me know the answers to important questions I had. During the divorce proceedings, I had a very good human lawyer, but he commented on how well I worked my own case. He didn't know that the Holy Spirit was telling me what to do every step of the way. I didn't know anything about law. I had never been to court before, but I had a very skilled Counselor with me, day in and day out.

If we take time each day to be quiet before the Lord, we can hear His still, small voice. (See 1 Kings 19:12 NKJV.) Seldom will we hear an audible voice, so we must be careful not to miss His still, small voice by dismissing anything that is not distinctly audible. And if we're whining, we're sure to miss His voice! God's regular communication with you depends upon how well you quiet yourself and listen to His Spirit.

The Holy Spirit is a Gentleman who gently leads and guides us. The devil pushes and shoves, but the Holy Spirit gently guides.

Teach me to do your will, for you are my God; may your good Spirit lead me on level ground. (Psalm 143:10)

Yes, the Holy Spirit will teach us, but we must be willing to learn. Yes, He will lead us, but we have to surrender to do His will. Our total surrender will make us winners and bring us into the presence and power of the Holy Spirit, and there's no greater fulfillment in life.

I want to encourage you to allow the Holy Spirit to raise up the winner within you daily. Yes, the enemy and our circumstances will invite us to whine. But the choice is yours, and I suggest that you decline to whine! The Lord will deal with you and me, but if we refuse to become winners, He will allow us to stay whiners. Let's not allow that to happen!

Chapter Twelve: From the Pit of Whining to the Peak of Winning

Points to Ponder

1. List some ways that you can recognize and distinguish between whiners and winners.

2. Are you generally a whiner or a winner? Even if you consider yourself a winner, in what areas might you still be a whiner?

3. Why are whiners easily derailed by disappointments, while winners are able to move on?

4. What is true success, as seen from God's point of view?

5. When we experience emotional and spiritual storms in our lives, we are often tempted to whine. What must we do instead, and how do we do it? In other words, how can we silence the whiner within?

Meditate on these Scriptures, speak them aloud, and commit them to memory.

For out of the overflow of the heart the mouth speaks.
(Matthew 12:34)

I can do all things through Christ who strengthens me.
(Philippians 4:13 NKJV)

Blessed is the man who trusts in the LORD, whose confidence is in him.
(Jeremiah 17:7)

Wait for the LORD; be strong and take heart and wait for the LORD.
(Psalm 27:14)

–13–

FROM THE PIT OF DEFEAT TO THE PEAK OF VICTORY

With the Lord God on our side, we are winners, for *"God…gives us the victory through our Lord Jesus Christ"* (1 Corinthians 15:57). Father doesn't want you wearing yourself out by trying to fight the financial, spiritual, emotional, or other battle that you are facing. The battle is the Lord's. (See 2 Chronicles 20:15.) As we cooperate with the Lord and use our provisions for defeating the enemy, we will experience victory in all areas of our lives. And this victory begins with our understanding the true battleground of the fight and not becoming preoccupied with minor skirmishes.

Knowing the True Battleground

Like all parents raising children, I've had to learn to focus on the larger picture of what is best for my daughter and to "pick my battles." Destiny has been a typical female since birth—she loves clothes and shoes. At a very early age, she started telling me what she did and did not want to wear. When Destiny was very young, yet old enough to form an opinion, I would set out two different outfits and let her choose which one she wanted to wear. It was a win-win situation: I was setting boundaries and saving my energy for more important battles, and Destiny felt like she had a say about what she was wearing.

As she has grown, I've had to change my strategies when choosing my battles. Destiny is now at the age when there are days she can wear whatever she wants to—of course, I don't allow her to buy any immodest, inappropriate clothing to begin with. But there are also days when I draw a tighter boundary. If Destiny is attending church or going somewhere with me to minister, I set more specific parameters to govern what she wears but still allow her to dress herself.

What would be the point in waging a war over what she wears? Even though I cringe sometimes to see her walk out of the house wearing her cousin's hand-me-downs when she has a closet full of newer clothing, it's not a battle I choose to fight. My greater concern is with what she watches on television, for example. I keep a tight rein on what she puts into her little spirit, because that's a fundamental battle I have to stay on top of.

In the same way that parents must learn to focus on the truly strategic battles when raising their children, we need to learn to focus on the strategic spiritual battles the Lord wants to fight on our behalf. The enemy loves to keep our attention focused on battles or little fires that aren't important but are intended to wear us out with stress and worry. If the devil can occupy us these more minor conflicts, he knows we won't have the time, energy, or attention to stay on guard during the battles that are crucial for us to deal with.

The Spiritual Battle for Hearts and Minds

One of those crucial battles is the battle over who will win our hearts and minds and the hearts and minds of our children—God, or the enemy? We must realize and deal with the atmosphere of spiritual warfare that surrounds our homes and our children. Unfortunately, many parents are too caught up in working in order to provide "stuff" for themselves and their children that they don't give their children the "stuff" they really need: time, love, attention, prayer, a listening ear, and godly guidance.

For example, I have learned that the older my daughter gets, the more she needs me. After a day at school, she needs to talk about what went on. When I pick her up, she gets in the car and talks all the way home. She tells me who said what that hurt her feelings. She tells me who kicked her in physical education class and what the girls did to the boys that day. She just needs to talk. She doesn't care if she's wearing hand-me-downs, but she does care if Mom's there to listen or not.

The Word of God tells us to *"encourage the oppressed. Defend the cause of the fatherless, plead the case of the widow"* (Isaiah 1:17). As members of the body of Christ, we *must* defend the cause of the fatherless. *To defend* means "to drive danger or attack away from." The number of fatherless or single-parent homes in our country is at an all-time high. The fatherless are left more vulnerable to the enemy, and their houses are left unprotected—unless there's someone standing in the gap and fighting a spiritual battle in prayer on their behalf. That's one of the greatest things we can give our children—prayer! Even children who are raised in single-parent homes can live healthy, successful lives when the covering of prayer surrounds them.

The Spiritual Battle of Priorities

The battle for our hearts and minds is closely related to the battle over what our priorities in life will be. For example, when my husband first moved out, the Lord taught me that any debt I incurred would require me to spend time away from my daughter, working to pay the bill. During this time, I learned that I could live more cheaply than I had ever imagined. I was motivated to prioritize my life wisely, and material goods weren't as important as my child's care.

The Lord said to me, "Be very frugal in your spending and very generous in your giving." As I walked in obedience, I was continually amazed. Was it easy? No way! Did I want to waver? Oh, yeah. At the end of each month, I could still see myself passing out stickers at Wal-Mart! But God would always encourage me and tell me that finances weren't a battle I had to fight. Even when I went to court concerning child support, the battle wasn't mine, but the victory was. God went before me and fought the battle for me. Remember, whatever the battle, it's not over until you and God win!

Empowered to Defeat Your Fears

Allowing the Lord to fight our battles for us involves defeating our fears, because fear always tries to control. If you fear that you won't have enough money, you will always try to control your finances. If you fear elevators, you will always try to control situations in order to bypass them. If you fear rejection, you will try to control your relationships in a way that prevents you from ever again experiencing the pain of rejection.

Yet when we face our fears by the power of the Holy Spirit and re-linquish control to the Lord, we can overcome any doubt and any fear, no matter how deeply rooted it is. The key is to surrender our control to the Lord. Things have to be out of our control in order for them to be in His control. And, when God is completely in control, we find ourselves in a great place. Sometimes, God "sets us up"—it's His way of helping us to surrender control to Him. If we need a lot of help, He'll allow everything to be out of our control, all at the same time. That's where I was on many occasions!

> **WHEN GOD IS COMPLETELY IN CONTROL, WE FIND OURSELVES IN A GREAT PLACE.**

On one of those occasions, it was that time again—the end of the month, when my mortgage payment was due. A friend of mine, Barbara, offered to watch Destiny so that I could spend the day trying to get some assistance with the payment. I did everything I knew to do, I went every-where I knew to go—and still nothing! At the end of the day, I pulled back into Barbara's driveway and put my van in park. I turned off the engine, threw my hands up in the air, and said, "Lord, either You've called me or You haven't! Either You're my Provider or You're not!" I was at the end of my rope. Everything was out of my control, but it was another setup from God. As I spoke those words out loud that day, something changed inside of me. I was at the end of myself, ready to surrender to-tally to the Lord.

After that day, things began to get easier because I had released ev-erything to the Lord. I began walking in faith instead of fear. As I walked in faith, things began to happen, and I even started to enjoy watching the miraculous hand of God provide for my daughter and me. After all, my "Daddy" owned it all!

Faith Is Your Title Deed

> Now faith is the assurance (the confirmation, the title deed) of the things [we] hope for, being the proof of things [we] do not see and the conviction of their reality [faith perceiving as real fact what is not revealed to the senses]. (Hebrews 11:1 AMP)

Your faith is your title deed to the answer to every need that you entrust to God! Your proof of ownership is in your title deed, so don't throw it away. When we operate in fear, we are throwing away our title deed—our faith. The real facts—what God says about the situation—are the truth. The facts that exist in the natural realm are often contrary to the real facts (the truth) that exist in the spirit realm. The real facts (truth) may not yet be revealed to the senses—the key words are *not yet*. As we stand in faith, the real facts will be manifested in the natural realm (or revealed to the senses).

> *Against all hope, Abraham in hope believed and so became the father of many nations, just as it had been said to him, "So shall your offspring be." Without weakening in his faith, he faced the fact that his body was as good as dead—since he was about a hundred years old—and that Sarah's womb was also dead. Yet he did not waver through unbelief regarding the promise of God, but was strengthened in his faith and gave glory to God, being fully persuaded that God had power to do what he had promised.* (Romans 4:18–21)

Against all hope in the natural realm or in the existing facts, Abraham hoped in the truth, believed, and so became the father of many nations. If our hope is in the natural facts, we'll have many opportunities to give up hope. But if, against all hope in the natural, we maintain hope in the truth of God's Word, we can believe and so become blessed with all of God's promises for our futures.

While we are standing in faith, it is crucial not to allow the enemy to mess with our emotions or thoughts. Continue speaking the Word concerning God's promises to you, and never throw away your title deed—your faith. Never allow an "if You can" or "if You will" attitude to come into your heart when you make requests of God.

The gospel of Mark gives the following account of a man who asked Jesus to heal his demon-possessed son.

> *Jesus asked the boy's father, "How long has he been like this?" "From childhood," he answered. "It has often thrown him into fire or water to kill him. But if you can do anything, take pity on us and help us." "'If you can'?" said Jesus. "Everything is possible for him who believes."* (Mark 9:21–23)

There is no such thing as "if You can" with the Lord. *All* things are possible—if we only believe. When we are operating in faith, we say, "Of course, God is going to do it." "Of course, God's provision will be there, as long as we are walking in total obedience."

Your Victory Is Sure When You Walk in Obedience

[God] *holds victory in store for the upright, he is a shield to those whose walk is blameless.* (Proverbs 2:7)

I kept walking in obedience to my Father—kept doing what I was called to do—and He kept on providing. Don't quit your job and go "live by faith" if Father didn't tell you to. If you quit your job and your house is going into foreclosure and you can't feed your kids, it probably wasn't God who told you to quit. If He leads you to do something, His provision will always be there. Learn from your mistakes, "grow forward," and get another job! Yes, God will supply all your needs, and He just may be waiting to use that job to do so.

> IF GOD LEADS YOU TO DO SOMETHING, HIS PROVISION WILL ALWAYS BE THERE.

With my title deed (my faith) in hand, I began listening to God's voice daily to hear *all* of His instructions. The key is *all*. I was desperate for God, so far out on a limb that I needed to hear God every day, in every little thing.

We sometimes get bits and pieces of what the Lord is saying in prayer, but we set out to do something before we hear all of the instructions. Often, when I tell my daughter to go to her room to clean it, she'll walk away before I have the opportunity to finish all of my instructions. We are often the same way with the Lord—we don't spend enough time in His presence to receive all of His instructions and equip ourselves with His winning strategies. There are other times when we are so anxious or excited that we run to do what we think He was saying, yet we miss some very important details.

Trust God, Even When His Battle Plan Sounds Illogical

After we hear our instructions from the Lord, we must allow the Holy Spirit to guard our minds and remain in peace. Isaiah 26:3 says, "*You will keep in perfect peace him whose mind is steadfast, because he trusts in you.*" We can't allow our minds to wander; instead, we must remained focused on God and what He has said. God will often give you seemingly illogical instructions that won't make sense to your natural mind. Don't worry—they don't have to. Father will keep you in perfect and constant peace as your mind stays on Him. In other words, park your mind in peace, put on the emergency brake, and don't allow your mind to shift into reverse!

As an umpire rules the plays in a game of baseball, peace is to rule the many decisions we make on a daily basis. Not the peace in our natural minds, but the peace in our spirits. The Lord can tell you to do something that makes no sense at all in the natural, yet in your spirit, you have peace about it if you're yielded to Him. There can be other times when your natural mind thinks, *I'd be crazy not to do this,* yet in your spirit, you don't have peace. Always allow the peace in your spirit to rule in every choice and decision. Remember, God sees the big picture.

The Battle for Peace of Mind

Father has made provision for us to have sound minds—minds that are worry-free, filled with peace, and renewed by the truth of God's Word. (See Romans 12:2.) When we accept Jesus Christ as our Lord and Savior and come to salvation through faith, we enter into a covenant relationship with God that entitles us to receive many covenant benefits, one of which is peace. However, our enemy, the devil, constantly seeks to rob us of our peace.

As young children, we have minimal control over our environments. We can't determine the atmosphere in which we are raised. But as we get older, we can choose to live life in a peaceful atmosphere. Those who were raised in chaotic environments often grow up "addicted" to chaos. It's the only way that they know how to function. Later on, though, they can come to know the truth that sets them free: God wants them to have peace that passes all understanding. In other words, we can have peace at all times, even when we can't possibly understand why we have peace in the midst of our circumstances.

Philippians 4:7 says, *"And the peace of God, which transcends all understanding, will guard your hearts and your minds in Christ Jesus."* Have you ever felt like you were losing your mind? Without the peace of Christ, everyone would feel that way, because it's the peace of God that guards our hearts and our minds. Don't let your guard down. Don't allow your guard, or your peace, to be stolen by the enemy, but pursue it with determination.

Pursue Peace

First Peter 3:11 instructs us to *"turn from evil and do good;...seek peace and pursue it."* We aren't supposed to simply *look for* or hope for peace, but we are to *chase it down* until we claim it for our lives. Claiming it happens when we allow the peace of God to be the umpire in our lives. The umpire makes the call. He calls what's inbounds and what's out-of-bounds.

"Let the peace of Christ rule in your hearts, since as members of one body you were called to peace. And be thankful" (Colossians 3:15). I have learned over the years never to make a choice or decision until I have peace. I don't have to understand why I have peace or why I don't have peace. I just have to allow the peace of Christ to rule—to call the shots—in my heart and in my life. As we pursue the peace of Christ, as we tap into this particular covenant benefit, our hearts and minds will be guarded. Then, and only then, will we enjoy all of the other covenant benefits that our heavenly Father has for us.

Renew Your Mind by Meditating on Things Above and Reading God's Word

A sound mind is not plagued with thoughts of fear, rejection, or other negative things, but it meditates instead on "things above." (See Colossians 3:2.) In other words, it meditates on truth, not the enemy's deceptions. Paul provided instructions on maintaining a sound mind in his letter to the church at Philippi:

> *Finally, brothers, whatever is true, whatever is noble, whatever is right, whatever is pure, whatever is lovely, whatever is admirable—if anything is excellent or praiseworthy—think about such things.*
> (Philippians 4:8)

Our greatest battles always begin in our minds. When the Lord started unpacking my emotional baggage, He showed me how closely my damaged emotions were connected to the thoughts that I had allowed the enemy to plague me with for many years. As we renew our minds daily with the truth of God's Word, we can maintain sound minds in the midst of every challenge life throws our way. God's Word is the answer key to every test in life—and, the good news is, it isn't considered cheating to use it!

Recognize the Enemy's Schemes

If we don't recognize the enemy's schemes, we can fall into traps. Paul wrote that we must do what is right in God's sight and maintain clear relationships with others, "*in order that Satan might not outwit us. For we are not unaware of his schemes*" (2 Corinthians 2:11).

If we are able to discern the tricks of the enemy, we can outwit him. If we stay on guard through prayer and meditation on the Word, Father will show us the schemes of the enemy. After a while, his schemes will become obvious. He doesn't have any new tricks; he only tries to catch us off guard with old tricks.

Reject the Enemy's Lies

A sound mind is hard to maintain when the devil makes his words echo in our ears on a daily basis. Do any of the following perceptions sound familiar?

+ *Nobody loves me.*
+ *I am all alone.*
+ *I'm different.*
+ *I don't have any friends.*

If so, you need to spend some significant time in God's Word. Your heavenly Father has given you a sound mind—a mind that is filled with the truth about you and your situation. Fill your mind daily with the truth of the Bible!

Speak, Think, and Do the Word Daily

In Joshua 1:8, we have this command: "*Do not let this Book of the Law depart from your mouth; meditate on it day and night, so that you may be careful to do everything written in it. Then you will be prosperous and success-ful.*" Father has given us the instruction, and it's up to us to carry it out. He has told us clearly how to be prosperous and successful. He has told us clearly that His desire is for us to have sound minds. Joshua 1:8 tells us not to "*let*" God's Word depart from our mouths. That means it's up to us. If we get lazy and "*let*" the words of the enemy fill our mouths, we have made a bad choice.

No one can choose for us. We must choose daily to speak the Word of God with our mouths. Again, the power of life and death is in our tongues. (See Proverbs 18:21.) Remember the power that Father said He has given us? (See, for example, Luke 10:19 KJV.) A lot of that power is right under our noses—in our tongues! We must speak the Word of God daily over ourselves and over our circumstances. Let's refuse to speak what the devil says and speak what the Word says instead!

Not only are we supposed to speak the Word, but we are also supposed to think and do the Word daily. Joshua 1:8 commands us to meditate on the Word day and night. In other words, we must think about the truth—God's Word. This verse also instructs us to fill our minds with the Word and be careful to do everything it says—basically, we are to *do* the Word. We need to *speak* the Word, *think* the Word, and *do* the Word. Say it out loud right now: "I need to speak the Word, think the Word, and do the Word. Daily, I need to speak the Word, think the Word, and do the Word!"

If we do those three things, we will repel fear and discouragement. James 4:7 tells us that if we resist the devil, he will flee from us. One way we resist the devil is by speaking, thinking, and doing the Word of God.

The Battle for Your Life

A mind that isn't sound is susceptible to believe the lies of the devil. If the devil gains the upper hand, one of his favorite tactics is to tempt people with thoughts of suicide. Maybe today, you feel as though you are in a deep, dark pit and can't get out. Don't let the enemy lie to you—suicide is not an option! Maybe you don't really want to die, but you just can't live the way you've been living any longer. Well, the good news is, you don't have to! Your heavenly Father is reaching out His arms of love to you today. By faith, you can grab hold of the rope of hope He is extending to you and determine to come out with victory.

If you have been battling thoughts of suicide—or if you know someone else who has—you must first understand that suicide is a spirit. This demon spirit is loosed from the pit of hell as part of Satan's attempt to do what he does best—steal, kill, and destroy. (See John 10:10.) Through suicide, the enemy steals from everyone affected by the loss of the individual who commits suicide—his or her children, other family members, friends, and coworkers. Our choices always affect those around us, and when we make a bad choice, everyone is affected in a negative way.

The lies of the enemy are always the opposite of the Word of truth—the Bible. Of the devil, the Bible says, *"He was a murderer from the beginning, not holding to the truth, for there is no truth in him. When he lies, he speaks his native language, for he is a liar and the father of lies"* (John 8:44).

The spirit of suicide comes with many lies and deceptions straight from the pit of hell. No pit that you find yourself in today is as bad as the pit of hell!

First of all, identify the lies that are attached to the spirit of suicide, such as:

+ *I'll be better off dead.*
+ *Everyone else will be better off without me.*
+ *Nobody really cares.*
+ *There's no other way out.*

Stand up and exercise the authority that has been given to you. Don't allow any demon from the pit of hell to push you around! It's time for you to start pushing the demon around. After all, you are the one with all of the authority, not he.

The lie is that there is no other way out. The truth is, you have a rope of hope just waiting to airlift you out, and Jesus is holding the other end. Refuse to entertain thoughts of suicide. You must bring captive every thought and make it obedient to Christ, as Paul wrote in 2 Corinthians 10:5: *"We demolish arguments and every pretension that sets itself up against the knowledge of God, and we take captive every thought to make it obedient to Christ."*

When we allow ourselves to sit around and dwell on the lies of the enemy, we open the door for the devil to have his way in our lives. But when we think on things above and not on things below, we open the door for the power and presence of God to consume us—and that's just what every one of us needs!

We must allow the evil deeds of darkness to be immediately exposed by the light.

> *Everyone who does evil hates the light, and will not come into the light for fear that his deeds will be exposed. But whoever lives by the truth comes into the light, so that it may be seen plainly that what he has done has been done through God.*   (John 3:20–21)

Allow the Holy Spirit to identify the lies, then speak to that spirit of suicide and command it to leave you or your loved one in the name of Jesus. You have all power and authority over Satan in the name of Jesus. We have this assurance in Luke 10:19: *"I have given you authority to trample on snakes and scorpions and to overcome all the power of the enemy; nothing will harm you."*

Don't sit in your pit and entertain thoughts from demonic spirits. Get up and go tell someone so he or she can pray with you and curse the spirit that's trying to take root in your life. If you don't have anyone close to you right now, you can call any number of national ministries with a twenty-four-hour prayer line. (See the list on page 251 for a few options.) And be encouraged! As you take that step of faith, your heavenly Father will meet you with open arms of love!

Remember Who the Real Enemy Is

As we go through our daily lives, we must know where the battles are coming from and identify the real enemy. If we don't identify the real enemy—Satan—we'll end up fighting with the people around us instead. Our battle is not with our family members, friends, coworkers, neighbors, or fellow church members. Although the enemy tries to use other people from time to time to instigate conflict, they aren't our enemies—the devil is.

For our struggle is not against flesh and blood, but against the rulers, against the authorities, against the powers of this dark world and against the spiritual forces of evil in the heavenly realms.

(Ephesians 6:12)

Well, there you go! That eliminates all those people whom we thought were the sources of our problems. They are in the *"flesh and blood"* category, so they are eliminated from the list of enemies against whom we struggle. Our struggle is not against them—get real! The struggle we are fighting is much greater than that. Our struggle is against the rulers, authorities, and powers of this dark world and the spiritual forces of evil in the heavenly realms, whose king is Satan.

You don't have to be an army general to know that in order to win a battle, you must fight against the real enemy. If you don't, you will be defeated. You will have your attention on someone else while the real enemy sneaks up behind you and blows you out of the water. You'll be destroyed before you know what hit you.

If we recognize the real enemy and fight with the weapons we have been instructed to fight with, we will be victorious every single time.

The weapons we fight with are not the weapons of the world. On the contrary, they have divine power to demolish strongholds.

(2 Corinthians 10:4)

What are the weapons of the world? The world's weapons are anger, bitterness, hatred, jealously, and backbiting. *"For though we live in the world, we do not wage war as the world does"* (2 Corinthians 10:3). Our battle tactics and weapons are quite different; *"they have divine power to demolish strongholds."* As we use our weapons of love, joy, peace, patience, kindness, goodness, faithfulness, gentleness, and self-control (see Galatians 5:22–23), they have divine power to demolish strongholds. Verse 5 of 2 Corinthians 10 goes on to specify what *"strongholds"* are: *"We demolish arguments and every pretension that sets itself up against the knowledge of God, and we take captive every thought to make it obedient to Christ"* (2 Corinthians 10:5).

Whatever stronghold we are fighting against, whether it's rejection, fear, suicide, or something else, it is a pretension that has set itself up against the knowledge of God. In other words, if we feel rejected, it's because of a pretension that the devil has set up against what God says about you and me. Father says we are loved and accepted by Him. The devil sets up "pretensions," which are defined as "allegations of doubtful value." He *pretends* things are true in order to get us to buy the lie.

His argument is, "No one loves you."

His pretension is, "You can't survive without that drug or without the acceptance and love from that special someone."

Those are lies from the pit! Yes, you are loved by God; yes, you can survive! Satan may put up arguments, but you cannot buy his lies. Don't fall for them! Take your spiritual weapons and destroy the devil's strongholds in your life!

Chapter Thirteen: From the Pit of Defeat to the Peak of Victory

Points to Ponder

1. List some battles that you are currently facing.

2. Now that you know that the battle is not yours but the Lord's, has your state of mind changed? How?

3. Explain how surrendering control to the Lord empowers us to defeat our fears.

4. Explain how faith is your title deed to the answer to every need that you give to God. (See Hebrews 11:1 AMP.)

5. The devil doesn't want you to walk in obedience to God. Explain why, based on what you have learned in this chapter.

6. What provision has God made for us to have sound minds?

Meditate on these Scriptures, speak them aloud, and commit them to memory.

The battle is not yours, but God's. (2 Chronicles 20:15)

But thanks be to God! He gives us the victory through our Lord Jesus Christ. (1 Corinthians 15:57)

Now faith is the assurance (the confirmation, the title deed) of the things [we] hope for, being the proof of things [we] do not see and the conviction of their reality [faith perceiving as real fact what is not revealed to the senses]. (Hebrews 11:1 AMP)

He holds victory in store for the upright, he is a shield to those whose walk is blameless, for he guards the course of the just and protects the way of his faithful ones. (Proverbs 2:7–8)

Everything is possible for him who believes. (Mark 9:23)

—14—

FROM THE PIT OF ADDICTION TO THE PEAK OF FREEDOM

Many different types of addiction plague society today. *Addiction* can be defined as "compulsive need for and use of a habit-forming substance." Addiction can also be the inclination or desire for a specific behavior or person in order to mask an undesirable emotional state, such as fear, anxiety, unbearable isolation, self-hatred, stress, and feelings of worthlessness, shame, inferiority, or inadequacy.

The pleasure experienced from the substance, behavior, or person temporarily displaces the pain. When the pain surfaces again, the addict chooses to engage in the pleasurable behavior once again to avoid the undesirable emotional state. Before long, the individual cannot function well without the pleasurable release, and thus an addiction is formed.

Honestly, most of us have addictions in some form or another. As I'm sitting in my study writing this chapter, I have an overwhelming desire for my favorite cookies. I want to drop everything and run across town to the bakery. The past two days, I've had to focus on writing and not allow my desire to derail me from my focus.

Some of our habitual inclinations are much more destructive than others because they result in enslavement to sinful behavior. The situation is a lot like what Paul described in Romans 7:15–25:

> *I do not understand what I do. For what I want to do I do not do,*
> *but what I hate I do. And if I do what I do not want to do, I agree*
> *that the law is good. As it is, it is no longer I myself who do it, but it*

is sin living in me. I know that nothing good lives in me, that is, in my sinful nature. For I have the desire to do what is good, but I cannot carry it out. For what I do is not the good I want to do; no, the evil I do not want to do—this I keep on doing. Now if I do what I do not want to do, it is no longer I who do it, but it is sin living in me that does it. So I find this law at work: When I want to do good, evil is right there with me. For in my inner being I delight in God's law; but I see another law at work in the members of my body, waging war against the law of my mind and making me a prisoner of the law of sin at work within my members. What a wretched man I am! Who will rescue me from this body of death? Thanks be to God—through Jesus Christ our Lord! (Romans 7:15–25)

Many people want to get out of the bondage of addiction but don't know how. Most of the time, they don't understand how the addictive behavior even started. Paul said, "*I…desire to do what is good, but I cannot carry it out.*" That is true for most addicts. And since they really desire to do what is good but can never seem to carry it out, the root of shame develops.

The Origins of Shame

The first chapter of Genesis tells us that God created man in His own image. (See verses 26–27.) Adam was placed in the garden of Eden to take care of it. Then, Eve was formed from Adam's rib because no other suitable helper was found for him. (See Genesis 2:15, 18–23.) Together, they were able to have their needs met through their union with each other and their communion with God. They felt no shame; they experienced no emotional brokenness or pain. They were good to go! Their every need was met by the Lord.

But after the fall of man—an act of disobedience through which Adam and Eve looked elsewhere for fulfillment rather than to God—everything was turned upside down. They looked outside of their relationships with God to have their needs met, and that's where the trouble began. It was a downward spiral that affected not only their lives but also the lives of all who would come after them.

Adam and Eve's act of disobedience caused them to experience the unpleasant emotion of shame. As a result of their shame, what did they do? They immediately tried to cover up their sin.

Then the eyes of both of them were opened, and they realized they were naked; so they sewed fig leaves together and made coverings for themselves. (Genesis 3:7)

That was phase one. Phase two of the big cover-up was their hiding.

Then the man and his wife heard the sound of the LORD *God as he was walking in the garden in the cool of the day, and they hid from the* LORD *God among the trees of the garden.* (verse 8)

It's easy for us to say, "It's not too smart to try to hide from God." But if we aren't careful, we'll do the same thing. Our sin nature wants to hide and cover up our sin and shame; it makes us resist confessing our sins to God and receiving His forgiveness.

Ensnared by the Fear of Shame

The very thing that keeps the addict bound to his addiction is his unwillingness to admit and confess his sin. Proverbs 28:13 says, "*He who conceals his sins does not prosper, but whoever confesses and renounces them finds mercy.*" In his fragile emotional state, the addict often views the admission of wrongdoing as a weakness that cannot be borne by his already poor sense of self-worth. Thus, his sense of shame deepens, and his desperation to find another source to blame increases.

Let's see how God responded when Adam and Eve hid from Him.

But the LORD *God called to the man, "Where are you?" He answered, "I heard you in the garden, and I was afraid because I was naked; so I hid." And he said, "Who told you that you were naked? Have you eaten from the tree that I commanded you not to eat from?"* (Genesis 3:9–11)

Adam didn't give a direct answer to the Lord's question. Instead, he shifted the blame to Eve! He said, "*The woman you put here with me—she gave me some fruit from the tree, and I ate it*" (verse 12).

Adam was really grasping for straws by this point. He even blamed God by saying, in effect, "That woman *You* put here with me? Yeah, that one. Well, it's really her fault, not mine. You're the one who put her here with me, so this was Your idea, not mine."

The actions of Adam and Eve are an example of how an addiction is birthed and how it affects many lives, not just the life of the addict. When people reach outside of the biblical boundaries established in Scripture, outside of their marital unions, and outside of their communion with the Lord to have their needs met, they are left empty and unfulfilled. The peace and fulfillment we desire can come only from intimacy with God. But sinful addictions separate us from God, leaving us with empty longings that can't be satisfied.

When our pursuit of a desire surpasses our pursuit of God, that desire has become an idol. All addictions serve as idols and take our focus and worship away from the Lord. The only way out of an addiction—the only way to receive true freedom from idolatry—is found in the words of Paul: "*Who will rescue me from this body of death? Thanks be to God—through Jesus Christ our Lord!*" (Romans 7:24–25).

Yes, deliverance comes only through Christ. It's not based on legalistic effort, but victory comes only through Christ our Lord. Yes, we are wretched, but Christ paid the price for our deliverance.

The Effects of Addiction

Sexual Addiction Is a Covenant Killer

To illustrate the effects of addiction, let us look at how sexual addiction can affect the addict and those closest to him or her. God designed the covenant of marriage to be between one woman and one man. Within that marriage covenant, the physical needs of each partner are to be met.

The husband should fulfill his marital duty to his wife, and likewise the wife to her husband. The wife's body does not belong to her alone but also to her husband. In the same way, the husband's body does not belong to him alone but also to his wife. Do not deprive each other except by mutual consent and for a time, so that you may devote yourselves to prayer. Then come together again so that Satan will not tempt you because of your lack of self-control.   (1 Corinthians 7:3–5)

When a marriage partner, whether the husband or the wife, receives physical satisfaction from self (masturbation), from images (pornography), or from an individual other than a spouse (adultery), he or she is looking outside of the marriage covenant to meet his or her sexual needs. I refer to sexual addiction as the covenant killer because it does just that—it kills the marriage covenant if it isn't acknowledged and dealt with.

Sexual addiction doesn't have to kill the covenant of marriage. There is hope for those bound by sexual addiction, as well as for those who are in relationships with addicted individuals. First and foremost, this hope comes from the Lord.

The Pain of Rejection

I can vividly remember the day when my suspicions about my husband's addiction were confirmed. As I've mentioned, during the first years of our marriage, I knew something was not right, yet I couldn't put my finger on it. My husband didn't seem as sexually interested in me as other husbands seemed with their wives. Time and time again, I thought that maybe our opposite work schedules were to blame. At other times, I concluded that something must be wrong—but what?

Whenever I questioned my husband about his behavior, he would come up with some excuse; if I pushed the issue, he would get verbally abusive. One night, after we had been married for a year or two, the Lord spoke to me in a dream. The dream was vivid as it described details of my husband's use of pornography. I woke up immediately afterward. Despite my previous suspicions, I was still shocked because I had repeatedly fallen into denial instead of facing the painful reality of what was happening in my marriage. That night, I sat up in bed and began yelling at my husband, who was asleep beside me. I was reacting, and I wouldn't advise anyone to handle the situation the way I did! I all but beat him over the head with my pillow. As I confronted him in anger, he continually denied my accusations, and I quickly slipped back into denial. I reacted first in anger and second by remaining in denial. A year went by before I began to act instead of react to the covenant killer that was destroying my marriage.

When I was six months pregnant, I found the first evidence that confirmed my suspicions. I could tell that pornography sites had been visited frequently on our home computer when the Web sites appeared on the monitor screen one day. Even after I confronted my husband with this information, he still denied his addiction! He sought to blame others instead of acknowledging his own brokenness. Although we were the only two people living in our home, he still insisted that he wasn't the one who had visited those sites.

Coming Out of Denial

Coming out of denial was one of the most painful processes I have ever experienced. Denial is a defense mechanism that we use to numb the pain of reality. When the anesthesia is taken away—when reality sets in—we experience in full the pain that had formerly gone unrecognized or unacknowledged.

Denial is defined as "refusal to admit the truth or reality; assertion that an allegation is false; refusal to acknowledge a person or thing." Denial, whether exercised by the addicted individual or by those in relationship with that individual, always proves destructive. But when we choose to face the facts about the situation, we can overcome it by the strength of the Lord. Once we allow the Holy Spirit to remove our carnal, fleshly attempts to deal with our pain, we are free to recognize and deal with the reality of things by the power, grace, and love of our heavenly Father.

> ABRAHAM WASN'T OVERWHELMED OR DISCOURAGED BY THE FACTS BECAUSE HE KNEW THE TRUTH OF GOD'S PROMISE WAS MUCH GREATER THAN THE FACTS.

Face the Facts with the Truth

When we choose to stay in denial, we are refusing to face the facts. The facts seem too overwhelming to deal with, so we opt not to recognize or believe them. A good biblical example of someone who faced the facts is Abraham. He wasn't overwhelmed or discouraged by the facts because He knew the truth of God's promise was much greater than the facts.

Without weakening in his faith, [Abraham] faced the fact that his body was as good as dead—since he was about a hundred years old—

and that Sarah's womb was also dead. Yet he did not waver through unbelief regarding the promise of God, but was strengthened in his faith and gave glory to God, being fully persuaded that God had power to do what he had promised. (Romans 4:19–21)

Again, the facts exist in the natural realm, but the truth exists in the supernatural realm. The truth (God's Word) always outweighs the facts. The fact may be that you just received a bad medical report. Your doctor may have given you four months to live. But be encouraged—those facts exist in the natural realm. The truth (God's Word) says that by Jesus' stripes, you were healed. (See Isaiah 53:5 NKJV.) It's already done. Don't buy the lie reported by the facts, but stand on the Word of truth. As you do this, you still must face the facts. If you stay in denial and refuse to face the facts, you can't change them. Facts can be changed to line up with the truth only when you are willing to face them and deal with them.

The fact may be that your spouse has a sexual addiction, but be encouraged by the truth of God's Word: *"If the Son sets you free, you will be free indeed"* (John 8:36). Father is just waiting to set you and your loved ones free, but you must be willing to face the fact that a problem exists.

Don't put off dealing with the problem. If your house were to catch fire, you would call the fire department as soon as you smelled smoke. You wouldn't wait until your house burned to the ground before calling 9-1-1. Every second you waited to call would increase the amount of destruction caused by the fire, and the same is true in other areas of our lives.

Just as Abraham faced the facts and held on to the truth of God's promises, being fully persuaded that God had the power to do what He had promised, you must stand on the truth today as you face the facts in your life. Be fully persuaded that God has all power to handle your situation. The Lord cannot be caught off guard. He knows about every situation long before you do. And He's not freaked out or shaken by them, so you don't need to be, either.

> THE LORD CANNOT BE CAUGHT OFF GUARD. HE KNOWS ABOUT EVERY SITUATION LONG BEFORE YOU DO. AND HE'S NEVER FREAKED OUT OR SHAKEN, SO YOU DON'T NEED TO BE, EITHER.

Acknowledging the Problem Gives You Access to Help

After being forced to face the facts, I slowly came out of denial by the grace and love of God. I don't believe I could have handled it any other way. When I found out about my husband's addiction, I had been in the ministry for fourteen years. In whom could I possibly confide? I thought, *Perhaps I shouldn't tell anyone. Maybe it would make matters worse if he found out I had discussed it with someone else.* The truth was, I had no idea of where to turn.

I decided to make an anonymous call to Focus on the Family to see if they would send me a book or some other material to help me during this time of crisis. Much to my surprise, they had only one book on the topic. I ordered the book and anxiously awaited its arrival.

Once it arrived, I immediately began reading. I still had not discussed the issue with anyone, but I was determined to get help in understanding what was going on in my marriage. As I read the first page, tears began flowing uncontrollably. I thought I would read a couple of chapters each day, but it didn't happen that way. When I read the author's testimony of being married to a man with a sexual addiction, I was painfully confronted with the truth of my own situation. I would read one page and then cry for two days. I was coming out of denial, and it was very painful—so painful that I had to take the truth in small doses. I would wait a day or two and then read another page, which would bring me a little further out of denial, and I would cry for another two days before I could read any more.

The book gave me understanding regarding my husband's behavior. It offered explanations for all the times he had disappeared, all the times he'd said he had to go to work early and had to stay late, all the times he'd wanted me to go out of town for a holiday without him, all the times he'd said he was at work and I'd later found out he hadn't been…all of it had been a bunch of lies to cover up his addiction.

Even though my husband refused to face and deal with the facts, I had to face them. I could no longer pretend there wasn't a problem; I couldn't deny my husband's addiction any longer. After slowly working my way through the heartrending yet enlightening book, I found a great Christian counselor who helped me sort things out.

Again, John 8:32 says, *"Then you will know the truth, and the truth will set you free."* I was set free as I came to acknowledge the truth of the situation. Yes, there was a problem. Yes, my marriage covenant was being broken. Denial keeps you in bondage, even if you aren't the one with the addiction. I was set free as the grace and power of God enabled me to embrace the truth.

Later on, I attended a class sponsored by Desert Stream Ministries. The class dealt with sexual addictions and helped addicts and their spouses alike. I would highly recommend the services of this worldwide ministry or another one like it to anyone suffering from any type of sexual addiction or sexual brokenness. Sexual addiction doesn't have to kill your marriage covenant. There is help available, but both marriage partners have to be willing to face the truth and deal with the issue, even when it hurts.

Dealing with Sexual Addiction

Sexual addiction is a persistent preoccupation with a fantasy, a behavior, or an emotional feeling of infatuation that often culminates in orgasm. This problem exists among men and women both in the church and outside of the body of Christ. Men often experience sexual addiction more erotically, with patterns of sexual behaviors, whereas women often experience more of an emotional addiction.

It has been said that some men play at love to get sex, and some women play at sex to get love. It's the feeling of pleasure from arousal and orgasm that sexually addicted men use to displace the undesirable pain in their lives. It's the so-called love that momentarily meets the deep longing for an emotional connection with someone that hooks the sexually addicted woman. Whether in males or females, sexual addiction can be broken only by the power of the Holy Spirit. The addiction stems from areas of hurt that the Lord alone can heal from needs that He alone can meet.

Acknowledge the Addiction

Breaking the cycle of addiction begins with the addict owning, or acknowledging, his state of brokenness. He can no longer blame everyone and everything else. He must acknowledge his need by admitting the emotional and erotic distortions that have resulted from his sexual broken-ness. Shame, guilt, and self-hatred can no longer prevent honesty concerning his need for deliverance. Only when the addict has owned his broken-ness is freedom within reach.

> But each one is tempted when, by his own evil desire, he is dragged away and enticed. Then, after desire has conceived, it gives birth to sin; and sin, when it is full-grown, gives birth to death. (James 1:14–15)

When the addict acknowledges that it's his own evil desire that has dragged him away and enticed him, he can stop the cycle leading him to spiritual and possibly physical death as a result of full-grown sin.

Bring the Addiction to Light

Addicts develop their addictions in darkness, and those addictions continue to thrive as long as they remain in darkness. The Word tells us that the evil deeds of darkness must be exposed under the light. As the light of truth shines on the evil deeds of darkness—the addiction—the addict can be set free. (See 1 John 1:5–2:1; John 3:19–21.)

Within the darkness of addiction, the addict develops an overwhelming sense of shame that further isolates him and reinforces his fear of the truth being revealed. His only hope of freedom is to allow others into his prison by letting the light of truth shine on his areas of darkness.

As the addict continues to reach for his freedom through his relationship with Christ, deliverance is assured. Still, there is the pain that must be faced in the process. After the addict admits his own brokenness to himself, God, and a few people he can trust, he must be willing to experience the pain he has been numbing for so long with his addictive behavior. He can no longer numb the pain with his addiction; rather, he must yield his pain to the Father. He must feel and deal. The addict employs behaviors that prevent him from feeling and thus from having to deal with the hurts and wounds from reality. When the addict allows himself to *feel*, he can then learn to *deal* with the pain by taking it to the Lord.

I have never struggled personally with a sexual or substance addiction, but I will never forget the heartrending pain that I experienced when coming out of denial about my husband's addiction. I had numbed myself with the carnal defense of denial for over two years, and when my "anesthesia" was taken away, I experienced all the pain that I had successfully covered up. The same is true for the addict. He must learn a whole new pattern of behavior when experiencing emotional pain—a pattern that's life-giving. He must exercise a pattern of running to Father and not running away from Him.

Understand the Addiction

As the addicted individual gains an understanding of the cycle of addiction, he can successfully break free and stay free. The first step in understanding the cycle of addiction is to learn what triggers his behavior. We have already established the fact that most addicts really don't want to be doing what they are doing, yet they are unable to stop the cycle by themselves. Yes, they need a higher power to help them—they need the Lord Jesus Christ to *carry* them to that place of total deliverance. It's the triggers that serve as launching pads, propelling the addicts into the behaviors they really don't want to do.

It's important that the addicted individual prays and asks the Holy Spirit to help him identify what triggers his addictive behavior. For most, it's the feeling of pain or stress, as mentioned earlier. When the addict stops and takes time to examine what's going on around him and how it relates to his own mind and emotions, he can identify his triggers. As the light of truth shines on the triggers, the addict comes another step closer to his freedom.

When the trigger occurs, the addicted individual is faced with a choice. He can fall into the addicted cycle and act out his lesser desire—the addictive behavior—or he can choose his greater desire, which is an intimate relationship with the Lord who meets all needs, heals all pain, and carries all burdens and stresses.

You Gotta Wantta

I always say, "You gotta wantta." In other words, you have to want your deliverance more than you want the temporary, momentary pleasure that the addictive behavior offers. Our choices are powerful. As addicts seek to break free from their addictions, they must think honestly about the consequences of their choices. Do they feel better and stronger after giving in to their addictive behaviors, or do they feel belittled and worthless, plunging deeper into a state of despair? Do they feel better equipped to face life's challenges, or have their actions only increased the challenges they now face? The answers to these questions really speak for themselves.

I have learned that the discipline (or the lack thereof) that I exercise in one area of my life affects my discipline (or the lack thereof) in every other area of my life. For instance, if I'm disciplined to get up early in the morning to exercise, it's easier for me to make disciplined choices in my eating habits for the rest of the day. But if I'm not disciplined in my exercise routine, I find that I'm less disciplined in other areas of my life, as well. I find that it's harder to be disciplined in one area if I have blown it in some other area.

As an individual faces the giant of addiction, his discipline or lack thereof in small areas of his life will affect him in the major areas. If he can say no to the lesser desires that have enslaved him, he can become empowered to resist even greater temptations.

Extra Motivation

Our ultimate motivation to make good choices should be our love for God and our desire to please Him. However, I don't believe it's wrong to be motivated by other things, as well—as long as the Lord is at the top of the list. After all, the Word says that there are blessings for obedience. (See Deuteronomy 28:1–13.) I don't believe it's wrong to reward good behavior; I believe it's scriptural to do so. When the reward is something that motivates a person, it can prove effective in establishing a pattern of desired behavior. We use this with our children all the time.

Several years ago, I was working with a young girl who struggled with an eating disorder. She had been through an intense program for bulimia treatment, through which she gained great understanding about what triggered her behavior. Much of her stress and emotional pain was healed, yet she would fall back into bulimia every couple of months if she was faced with various triggers. I went to the Lord in prayer for her because everything within me cried out, *She has to get totally free and stay free!*

When I cried out to the Lord on her behalf, the Lord said to me, "She's motivated by money."

I said, "Okay, what does that have to do with her eating disorder?"

The Lord went on to tell me to use what motivated her to help her get over this hump, once and for all. So, I told her that every time she purged her food, she would have to pay me; every time she made it a month without purging, I would pay her. If she purged the first month, she would have to pay me $100, and if she made it through a whole month without purging, I would pay her $100. Each month, the amount of money would increase—the second month, the purging fine would be $200, and the reward would also be $200. I told her that we were going to do this for six months, with the amounts increasing each month. She had a chance to earn $2,100 over the six-month period.

She never purged again, and, to this day, she is totally free from the addiction of bulimia! She was motivated and blessed with a bundle of money and total freedom from a behavior that had kept her bound for many years. God is good! This girl really wanted to get free, and when she was motivated by something positive—money—she overcame bulimia for good.

Receive God's Grace, Which Fulfills More than Any Addictive Behavior

As we draw near to God, He will draw near to us (see James 4:8 NKJV), and soon, the grace of the Father will begin to flow in our lives. His grace is always sufficient for us. (See 2 Corinthians 12:9.) As we draw near to Him by yielding our hearts and wills to Him, we begin to long for His presence. We want to read and meditate on the Word, pray, and worship. We all have been created to worship Him—that's our hearts' true desire. And if we continually draw near to Him, it gets easier and easier to make life-giving choices. As this happens, our desires for lesser things begin to fade away.

When we are faithful to devote time to the Father, we experience the presence and power of the great I Am. He is our peace. He is our joy. He is our contentment, our love, and our everything! Before long, the great I Am will have turned our stumbling blocks into stepping stones.

After Jesus ascended into heaven, He sent the Holy Spirit to be with His children. The Holy Spirit is our Counselor, Comforter, and Teacher who leads us and guides us into all truth. (See John 16:7, 13.) He leads us into what to do and what not to do. *"The Spirit helps us in our weaknesses"* (Romans 8:26) and enables us to be strong and courageous. We all need the power and presence of the Holy Spirit in our lives. When we go through difficult times, we have the privilege of being able to rely on the Holy Spirit 100 percent. It's really a blessing when the Lord allows us opportunities to trust Him. And always remember—tough times don't last, but tough people do!

Hold On to Hope

Addiction is a type of bondage, but you don't have to be a slave to it any longer. Now that you understand the cycle of addiction, you must understand that achieving deliverance and freedom is a process. In the seventh chapter of Romans, Paul wrote, *"I do not understand what I do. For what I want to do I do not do, but what I hate I do"* (verse 15). He continued with his description of being bound by his sinful nature yet wanting to do the right thing. Then, he came to the following conclusion:

> *Therefore, there is now no condemnation for those who are in Christ Jesus, because through Christ Jesus the law of the Spirit of life set me free from the law of sin and death.* (Romans 8:1–2)

In other words, don't condemn yourself or put yourself down, but understand that deliverance is a process. God's grace is not a license to sin, but His grace extends forgiveness to those who are really trying to live out their commitment to Christ.

I can remember my first year as a born-again Christian. I was seventeen years old, a senior in high school. For the first year, I slipped and slid in my relationship and commitment to Christ. I did my very best to walk out my commitment, and I never turned my back on the Lord. I learned to say no to the flesh while strengthening my spirit. Looking back, I know that God knew my heart. My heart was right, yet my actions were not always in line with my heart. After the first year, things got a lot easier, and, by the grace of God, I kept running hard after Him.

A little later in Romans 8, Paul shared some helpful advice for those who want to do the right thing.

Those who live according to the sinful nature have their minds set on what that nature desires; but those who live in accordance with the Spirit have their minds set on what the Spirit desires. The mind of sinful man is death, but the mind controlled by the Spirit is life and peace. (verses 5–6)

Your mind plays a big part in determining your actions. What is your mind set on? If you allow your mind to be set on ungodly, perverted things, the Word says that it will result in death. The mind that is controlled by the Spirit of the Lord, on the other hand, brings life and peace.

As you maintain your devotional life with the Lord through prayer, Bible study, and worship, your mind becomes renewed by the truth. This fulfills the apostle Paul's instruction to *"be transformed by the renewing of your mind"* (Romans 12:2). When your natural mind wants to wander to ungodly thoughts that don't bring about the life of Christ in your life, begin to speak the Word of God aloud. Don't just think about the Word, but boldly speak it out loud! Recite proclamations based on Scripture, such as:

+ "I have the mind of Christ." (See Philippians 2:5 NKJV; 1 Corinthians 2:16.)

+ "I think on things above, not things below." (See Colossians 3:2.)

+ "Thank You, Lord, that my mind is washed by the water of Your Word." (See Ephesians 5:25–26.)

The power of life and death is in your tongue (see Proverbs 18:21), so speak life over yourself. As you speak the Word, you also hear it with your ears. Before long, the desire for the lesser will fade away, and your spirit will be bold and strong. The mind that's controlled by the Spirit is life and peace, remember? (See Romans 8:6.)

Who shall separate us from the love of Christ? Shall trouble or hardship or persecution or famine or nakedness or danger or sword?…No, in all these things we are more than conquerors through him who loved us. (Romans 8:35, 37)

Nothing can separate us from Christ and His love for us—no difficult time, no addiction, no trial, no hardship. As a matter of fact, Father will use those times to show Himself all-powerful in our lives. He will use those times to let us know and experience His love in our lives as never before. What's not God-sent will be God-used—if we just run to Him.

And we know that in all things God works for the good of those who love him, who have been called according to his purpose.

(Romans 8:28)

No, God isn't the author of the bad things that happen in our lives, but His Word does say that He will work all things together for our good if we just keep our hearts right and don't allow bitterness, anger, and unforgiveness to take root there.

When Your Loved One Is an Addict

If you are the spouse or friend of an addict, it will be useful for you to learn how to act and not react to the individual's addiction. Many times, I have seen a woman react to her husband's addiction by falling into some ungodly pattern of behavior of her own. I have known women who, out of their deep pain of rejection, have allowed themselves to get involved in an illicit relationship. Some have even developed their own sexual addictions. Many have turned to drugs and alcohol or have become exotic dancers.

Even we who are not addicts must run to Christ, too. We must place our pain at the foot of the cross and allow Father to heal our wounds. We must not react by leading lives of brokenness ourselves. Rather, we need to take action that is life-giving for both us and our children. We must make sure that our choices are inspired by the Holy Spirit, which assures us that our choices are within the will of God. This includes all of our choices and decisions, large and small.

Provide a Safe Environment of Unconditional Love

It is important to provide a place where the addicted individual can be healed—a place of safety, where the individual can admit and deal honestly with his problem with assurance of complete confidentiality. A safe environment offers unconditional love and the promise that any information disclosed will not be repeated. When confidentiality is maintained, trust can be built, enabling the addicted individual to feel comfortable enough to open up and share from the depths of his heart. I cannot stress enough the importance of confidentiality. Honesty is a vital key to the addict's deliverance, but without the assurance of confidentiality, he will likely choose not to disclose information.

The crucial element of unconditional love also extends forgiveness to the addict, who often has hurt and wounded those closest to him. Our choice to forgive and release the person is vital to his healthy recovery—and to our own healthy growth, as well. Unforgiveness is a deadly trap that none of us can afford to fall into, but when we forgive and release those who have hurt and wounded us, we are free to come into all that Father has for us—the abundant life of joy, peace, and true fulfillment.

Chapter Fourteen: From the Pit of Addiction to the Peak of Freedom

Points to Ponder

1. Read Romans 7:15–8:2 and explain why these verses give us hope.

2. What is the very thing that will keep an addict bound to his addiction?

3. Why does acknowledging an addiction help in breaking the cycle of addiction?

4. In this chapter, I refer to sexual addiction as a covenant killer. Explain why this is an apt term for that type of addiction.

5. Your mind plays a big part in determining your actions. Why do you think this is true? What can you do to renew your mind?

Meditate on these Scriptures, speak them aloud, and commit them to memory.

He who conceals his sins does not prosper, but whoever confesses and renounces them finds mercy. (Proverbs 28:13)

God cannot be tempted by evil, nor does he tempt anyone; but each one is tempted when, by his own evil desire, he is dragged away and enticed. Then, after desire has conceived, it gives birth to sin; and sin, when it is full-grown, gives birth to death. (James 1:13–15)

If we claim to be without sin, we deceive ourselves and the truth is not in us. If we confess our sins, he is faithful and just and will forgive us our sins and purify us from all unrighteousness. (1 John 1:8–9)

Those who live according to the sinful nature have their minds set on what that nature desires; but those who live in accordance with the Spirit have their minds set on what the Spirit desires. The mind of sinful man is death, but the mind controlled by the Spirit is life and peace. (Romans 8:5–6)

—15—

From the Pit of Unforgiveness to the Peak of Reconciliation

The process of forgiving my father took much longer than I ever thought it would. I had thought that when I said, "Okay, I forgive my dad," it would be over. But I couldn't stop there. Over a period of several years, the Lord showed me things in my heart, and I continually had to choose to forgive. When we feel rejected, the feeling is often rooted in pride, and when we hold on to unforgiveness, it reveals a self-centered heart attitude that says, *What about me? What about my pain? It's all about me!* Unforgiveness refuses to look at the pain of those who hurt us and focuses only on our own pain. This is the exact opposite of Christ's example.

I learned that in every situation, we must be willing to acknowledge the pain that others are experiencing. When my parents divorced, I didn't realize all the pain my father was going through; I could see only my pain. When my husband left our marriage due to his sexual addiction, I couldn't see all the emotional pain he was in. I couldn't see past my own devastating pain of rejection. I couldn't acknowledge at the time the terrible pain he was dealing with.

Bitterness always looks at the bad; it dwells on the mistakes of others. Love, on the other hand, always looks at the good. The Lord revealed to me that my dad had given me the best thing a father could ever give a child: the opportunity to accept Christ into my life as my Savior. My dad had been the one who had taken me to church when I'd gotten saved, and the gratitude I felt toward him helped me to forgive him. In many ways, God used my dad to totally change my life! Still, learning to forgive was a long and difficult process.

When I first became a Christian, I thought that I would no longer have any problems. I thought that life would be free from emotional pain because I had chosen to serve Christ. Well, I quickly learned that what I thought wasn't reality. Look at what God's Word tells us: *"Many are the afflictions of the righteous"* (Psalm 34:19 NKJV).

The dictionary defines *affliction* as "the cause of persistent pain or distress; great suffering." Yes, even as believers, we face painful circumstances that cause us distress and suffering. But it's how we react to the afflictions that really counts. It's not *what* you go through in life that matters—it's *how* you go through it. Going through great trials and difficult circumstances in life doesn't disqualify us from God's plan—but how we go through them might! We must never forget the second part of Psalm 34:19: *"But the LORD delivers him out of them all"* (NKJV).

We can choose to grumble and complain. We can choose to hold grudges against God and others. We can choose to have a pity party and invite everyone we know to join us in our misery. We can choose to get bitter and harbor unforgiveness in our hearts toward others. Or, we can choose to let go of offenses and let the river of God's mercy flow in our lives. When we choose the latter course, we experience joy unspeakable and the fullness of His glory (see 1 Peter 1:7–8 KJV), in spite of life's many trials and heartaches.

> WE CAN CHOOSE TO LET GO OF OFFENSES AND LET THE RIVER OF GOD'S MERCY FLOW IN OUR LIVES.

Forgive, and You Will Be Forgiven

One clear command that we are given in the Word of God is to forgive. Jesus said, *"If you forgive men when they sin against you, your heavenly Father will also forgive you"* (Matthew 6:14). Paul reinforced this command of Jesus in Colossians 3:13: *"Bear with each other and forgive whatever grievances you may have against one another. Forgive as the Lord forgave you."*

If we aren't careful, sometimes we can be "bears" with one another when it comes to grievances and differences. We growl, we attack—we basically act like bears toward others instead of being patient with them and forgiving whatever grievances we may have against them. Notice that in the above verse, the word *"whatever"* precedes the word *"grievances."* Just in case you think your situation is an exception, the Lord included the word *whatever*—and that includes your *whatever*, too!

There is nothing for which the Lord won't forgive us, and there is nothing for which we aren't expected to forgive others. Murder, child molestation, adultery—whatever the grievance, we must forgive! And if we don't, there are serious consequences.

> *For if you forgive men when they sin against you, your heavenly Father will also forgive you. But if you do not forgive men their sins, your Father will not forgive your sins.* (Matthew 6:14–15)

That's serious. God says what He means, and He means what He says.

In our society today, many people have a hard time respecting and obeying authority figures. It often begins during the early stages of life. Children are notorious for pushing the limits and testing the boundaries. They like to see how much they can get away with.

One day, I was driving with Destiny, a toddler at the time, and she was playing with her stuffed animals in the backseat. She usually put her stuffed animals in "time-out" for "disobeying," but this particular day, she made a comment that caught my attention. As she corrected her toy dogs, I heard her say, "He gets two chances to listen." My ears perked up—children's play often reflects their own experiences and perceptions—and I immediately thought, *I need to tighten up the ship. She doesn't believe that I mean what I say the first time.* I had never told her that she had two chances to listen, but my actions must have communicated that to her loud and clear. If our children grow up concluding that Mommy and Daddy don't really mean what they say the first time, they develop a pattern of pushing the boundaries. The pattern carries into their adult lives, when they'll conclude, for example, that a speed limit of fifty-five miles per hour really means sixty-five or seventy miles per hour. Sound familiar?

Many people push the boundaries even in their walks with the Lord. Don't try to see how much you can get away with; don't try to see how far you can push the envelope with the Lord. God says what He means, and

He means what He says the first time. If we don't forgive others, He can't forgive us of our sins. That's a big, important *if*. We all face this very crucial choice at some point in our lives—and it is a choice. Choose to obey. Choose to forgive.

How You React to Offense Determines Your Destiny

Again, Jesus said that we will inevitably experience offenses. (See Luke 17:1 NKJV; John 16:33.) It's what you do with the offenses that will determine your destiny. Offense, at the beginning level, is not harmful—as long as you don't deny your hurt feelings. Don't "stuff it" and pretend everything is all right. Deal with it in a godly manner—the proper reaction to offense. Like it or not, your reaction will determine your destiny!

> *If an enemy were insulting me, I could endure it; if a foe were raising himself against me, I could hide from him. But it is you, a man like myself, my companion, my close friend, with whom I once enjoyed sweet fellowship as we walked with the throng at the house of God.*
> (Psalm 55:12–14)

When those closest to us hurt and offend us, we feel a deep sense of betrayal. The closer the relationship, the more painful the offense. History shows us that the bloodiest wars were civil wars. Any police officer will tell you that some of the most dangerous calls the police respond to are domestic disputes. Those you care about the most can hurt you the most. You expect more from them—after all, you've given them more of yourself. Yes, the pain is greater from those closest to us, yet the biblical command remains the same: forgive, and you will be forgiven.

Offended people can be divided into two categories: those who have been mistreated and those who *believe* they have been mistreated. As we discussed earlier, your offense can be a perception deception straight from the pit of hell. We sometimes draw conclusions based on inaccurate information by assumption, appearance, or hearsay.

Even if you have been mistreated, remember that when you hold on to the offense and refuse to forgive, the only person you are hurting is yourself!

Pull Up the Root of Bitterness

Make every effort to live in peace with all men and to be holy; without holiness no one will see the Lord. See to it that no one misses the grace of God and that no bitter root grows up to cause trouble and defile many.   (Hebrews 12:14–15)

Bitterness is a root. If roots are cared for or nursed—watered and given nutrients and sunlight—they grow. They get deeper and stronger. Moreover, if you don't deal with the roots of unwanted plants quickly, they get harder to pull up. Remember my saying? Don't nurse it, don't rehearse it, just curse it in the name of Jesus. Don't nurse that root of bitterness by harboring it in your mind or feeling sorry for yourself and focusing on your emotional pain. Don't rehearse it by repeating over and over in your mind or out loud how much something or someone hurt you. Don't nurse it, don't rehearse it; just curse it at the root in the name of Jesus.

The Word says that a bitter root grows up to *"cause trouble and defile many."* If a root of bitterness is left to grow, it will do so quickly, not only causing trouble for you, but also defiling or contaminating others. How? It grows to defile many because your carnal nature wants to rehash your hurt over and over again. You rehearse it in your mind, and then you rehearse it by telling anyone who will listen all about it. You talk about how unfairly you were treated and enumerate all the awful things that were done to you: "Poor old me; I was so mistreated."

You rehearse it so much that even those around you get tired of hearing it, and they let you know it, either verbally or nonverbally. Still, you continue to rehearse it. By the time it gets to this stage, a deeper level of self-pity sets in. Now you say, "No one even cares how hurt I was." It's not that others don't care; it's that they're sick of hearing about it. Don't poison those around you by rehearsing your offenses. Don't share your bitter root with them. Don't rehearse it; just curse it in the name of Jesus. Take it to the Lord and leave it at the foot of the cross, releasing those who have hurt you.

Stop Believing You Have the Right to Be Bitter

The enemy loves to deceive people and keep them from knowing the truth. Deception is a terrible thing because the one being deceived often believes with all of his heart that he is right. It's important that we know the truth concerning the conditions of our hearts before the Lord.

None of us ever has the "right" to hold on to offenses and unforgiveness in his heart. No matter what anyone has done to you or hasn't done to you, you must forgive. Again, even in the most horrendous circumstances and situations, we never have the right to harbor unforgiveness in our hearts.

Several years ago, I was awakened by a startling dream. In the dream, a person whom I knew and loved had died. When that person died, she began traveling through this long, dark tunnel into eternity. Much to my surprise, there was no light at the end of the tunnel—only darkness. Still dreaming, I said, "That doesn't look like heaven, Lord. She was a Christian, and went to church every Sunday."

The Lord responded, "Yes, but she had unforgiveness in her heart toward _____," and He said the name of a lady. Then, I woke up. I was so shaken! I knew the Lord was saying that my friend was going to die, and that if she died today, she would not go to heaven due to the unforgiveness in her heart.

I prayed and I prayed, asking the Lord for an open door to share my dream with this dear lady whom I deeply loved. God is so faithful—He opened a door, and I was able to tell her about the dream and name the person against whom she had unforgiveness. She immediately prayed with me with a humble heart of repentance. I gave her the book *The Bait of Satan* by John Bevere. She read the entire book and thanked me. It wasn't too long afterward that she went to be with the Lord. I was so glad that I had obeyed His leading.

Unforgiveness can be a deadly deception if it's allowed to stay in our hearts. Don't allow yourself to be deceived into thinking that you have a right to be offended. Don't allow the deadly deception of unforgiveness to prevent you from spending eternity with the Lord. We must forgive others if we want to receive forgiveness from our heavenly Father for our sins against Him. (See, for example, Matthew 6:12, 14–15.)

I want to strongly encourage you right now to ask the Lord if there is any unforgiveness in your heart toward anyone. Ask Him to reveal any strongholds of offense that may be trying to take root in your life. This is an important issue to address. Address it immediately—right now! If the Lord reveals any unforgiveness or offenses, repent and release those individuals right now. Nothing is of greater importance. Your eternal destiny could be dependent upon the decision you make today!

Adopt the Mind-set of Forgiveness

Forgiveness starts with the right mind-set, and unforgiveness starts with a wrong mind-set. The third chapter of Colossians gives us guidelines for living a holy, godly life, which includes forgiveness.

Set Your Mind on the Word of Truth

Set your hearts on things above, where Christ is seated at the right hand of God. Set your minds on things above, not on earthly things. For you died, and your life is now hidden with Christ in God. When Christ, who is your life, appears, then you also will appear with him in glory. Put to death, therefore, whatever belongs to your earthly nature: sexual immorality, impurity, lust, evil desires and greed, which is idolatry. Because of these, the wrath of God is coming. You used to walk in these ways, in the life you once lived. But now you must rid yourselves of all such things as these: anger, rage, malice, slander, and filthy language from your lips. Do not lie to each other, since you have taken off your old self with its practices and have put on the new self, which is being renewed in knowledge in the image of its Creator. Here there is no Greek or Jew, circumcised or uncircumcised, barbarian, Scythian, slave or free, but Christ is all, and is in all. Therefore, as God's chosen people, holy and dearly loved, clothe yourselves with compassion, kindness, humility, gentleness and patience. Bear with each other and forgive whatever grievances you may have against one another. Forgive as the Lord forgave you. And over all these virtues put on love, which binds them all together in perfect unity. Let the peace of Christ rule in your hearts, since as members of one body you were called to peace. And be thankful. (Colossians 3:1–15)

This passage begins, "*Set your hearts*…[and] *your minds.*" Thus, this is a choice we make, and it requires action on our part. We choose to "set our minds" on things above.

Wherever you set your mind determines your mind-set, and all of your choices and decisions flow from your mind-set. You see and perceive things through your mind-set, so you have to be extremely careful where you set your mind. No one can set your mind for you. I can set your glass down for you, I can set your books across the room on the shelf for you, I can set your car keys on the counter, but I can't set your mind anywhere for you.

Some people set their minds ten years ago, when words were spoken over them that formed their mind-sets. Others set their minds fifteen or twenty years back, when someone did something to them and thereby formed the mind-sets in which they now operate.

We must set our minds on things above—on the Word of truth. As we meditate on the Word of God, our minds will be set on things above and not on things below. Someone may have said or done things that deeply wounded you, but don't set your mind there. If you set your mind on all the things that have hurt you, you may develop the mind-set of a victim and continually live out of that mind-set of offense and pain.

Our lives are affected greatly by our mind-sets. Have you ever heard someone say, "I feel like I'm losing my mind"? Well, when someone sets his mind on a situation or circumstance by meditating on it continually, he may feel as though he is losing his mind, because his mind has been set on the situation and is no longer set on things above. In a sense, he has lost his mind to the lies of the enemy and to meditation on unpleasant circumstances.

Rid Yourself of a Bitter Attitude

But now you must rid yourselves of all such things as these: anger, rage, malice, slander, and filthy language from your lips. (Colossians 3:8)

The Word says, "*now you must rid yourselves.*" Don't delay; you can't afford to wait. If we wait to rid ourselves of ungodly heart attitudes and actions, we open the door for the enemy to develop a stronghold of bitterness and unforgiveness in our hearts. Daily, we must humble ourselves before the Lord and ask Him to purify our hearts. The Holy Spirit is ready and willing to reveal to us any bitterness or unforgiveness that may be trying to take root in our lives. The longer we hang on to an offense, the deeper the roots become. The deeper the roots, the harder it is to get the offense out of our lives.

Again, *we* must rid *ourselves* of the negative things Paul listed; no one can do it for us. It takes action on our part—not by our might or power, but by our relying on the power of the Holy Spirit. (See Zechariah 4:6.) Our action begins with our willingness to rid ourselves of anger, rage, malice, and so forth. After we have willingly repented before the Lord, the Holy Spirit is right there to help us carry out the will of the Father—forgiving and releasing others.

Paul's words make clear that we *must* rid ourselves of all such things. In other words, we don't have a choice. There's no way around it. If we want to please the Lord, if we want to be in right standing with the Father, then we must rid ourselves of ungodly emotions and improper heart attitudes. *To rid* means "to make free; relieve, disencumber." We rid ourselves of evil by setting our minds on the Word, confessing our sins, repenting, praying, and worshipping.

Let Go and Let the River Flow

Forgiveness entails letting go. Yet, letting go of an offense or a hurt is not a natural response for our flesh. The flesh's natural response is to get even by inflicting pain on those who have caused us pain. This response does not bring honor to God, obviously!

Letting go of yesterday and releasing the individuals who have caused us pain begins with a choice: the choice to forgive. The process of releasing offenses and extending forgiveness to others is completed successfully when we choose daily to walk in forgiveness.

Only after we choose to let go of yesterday can the river of God's presence flow freely in our lives today. Psalm 46:4 says, "*There is a river whose streams make glad the city of God, the holy place where the Most High dwells*" (Psalm 46:4). In this verse, the river can be seen as a metaphor for the continual outpouring of God's blessings, which sustain and refresh us like water for the soul. If we refuse to give unforgiveness a place in our hearts,

GOD'S BLESSINGS SUSTAIN AND REFRESH US LIKE WATER FOR THE SOUL.

we can truly experience the continual outpouring of God's blessings and His refreshing presence.

Extend Forgiveness and Receive God's Peace

Isaiah 66:12 expresses a promise made by God: *"I will extend peace to her like a river."* Peace and righteousness go hand in hand throughout the Scriptures. When we walk in righteousness and do the right thing before God, peace is extended to us—a *river* of peace. But when we harbor unforgiveness in our hearts, we throw away one of the covenant benefits we discussed before—peace. Have you ever noticed that bitter people don't have a lot of peace? They stir things up wherever they go because they don't want others to have peace, either. Bitterness and unforgiveness have stolen their peace.

Father has made His peace available to us, but we must obey His Word by forgiving others in order to partake of this covenant benefit. Isaiah 48:18 says, *"If only you had paid attention to my commands, your peace would have been like a river, your righteousness like the waves of the sea."* If we obey Father's command to forgive others, we will experience His peace that passes all understanding.

> FATHER HAS MADE HIS PEACE AVAILABLE TO US, PEACE THAT PASSES ALL UNDERSTANDING.

Examine Your Heart

Is the river of God's peace flowing in your heart and life today? If not, maybe there's some junk in your river. One day, I was traveling and passed what appeared to be a beautiful river. As I continued to drive, I got a closer look. Glancing out my window, I could see junk floating in the water. There were broken tree limbs, old tires, aluminum cans, and other trash and debris. The river that had first appeared so beautiful suddenly lost its beauty when I saw it up close.

Later, the Lord spoke to me and said, "That's how My children are when they have unforgiveness in their hearts—they have junk floating in their rivers." We must let go and let the river of God's presence flow in our lives. Not only does junk in the rivers of our hearts take away the beauty of God's presence in our lives, but it also stops us from flowing with the power that comes from His presence. For the river of God's presence to flow freely in our lives, and for us to extend forgiveness to others who have hurt us, it takes "soul control."

Soul Control

For the first seventeen years of my life, my soul and my flesh were in control. After I accepted Christ into my life as my Lord and Savior, the Holy Spirit began to teach me that my renewed spirit was now to be the one in control. And my spirit needed to be under the control of the Holy Spirit.

Our souls include our wills, emotions, and natural minds. The night I got saved, my spirit was immediately restored to its proper place with God, but my soul realm had not yet changed. I was about to learn that this transformation was going to be a process. Since my soul and my flesh had been in control for seventeen years, I was controlled by what I wanted (my will), what I thought (my natural mind), and how I felt (my emotions).

If we truthfully answer the question, "Do you have soul control?" most of us would have to say, "Some of the time," or "In some situations." When we don't have our souls under the control of our renewed spirits, they control us. In other words, it's all about what we want, what we think, and how we feel.

Our spirits want to do the will of the Father, and they long for fellowship with the Lord. Our spirits desire to do what is righteous and to follow the commands of the Lord. But getting our souls and our flesh in agreement with our spirits takes some effort. Our spirits want to forgive and to walk in love. But then, we have our natural minds saying, *Forgive her? You must be crazy. Don't you remember what she did to you? You have a right to be angry.* Then, our emotions jump in the middle of things as we remember how hurt we were:

+ *I felt rejected.*

+ *I felt unloved.*

+ *I felt left out.*

In the soul realm, it's all about self. When you die to self and follow Christ, it's no longer about self; it's about Christ.

When we get our minds, our wills, and our emotions in line with our spirits, nothing can stop us from experiencing all the blessings of the Lord. There are always blessings on the other side of obedience. Many times, the Holy Spirit has led me to do things that went against what my natural mind thought should be done. I had to choose to get my mind in agreement with my spirit. Each time that I did, I looked back and thanked God that I had followed the leading of the Holy Spirit.

When the Lord said, "Now is the time to start your television ministry," my mind said, *You must be kidding!* When the Lord told me to move our administrative offices into a much larger facility, my mind said, *We need more partners before we can do that.* As we maintain soul control, we can be led by the Holy Spirit. The Holy Spirit will lead us and guide us into all truth—truth about how to handle every situation and truth about our own hearts' conditions.

The Process of Forgiveness

Acknowledge You've Been Hurt

The first step toward healing and freedom from offenses is to admit that you have been hurt. Many Christians deny and repress hurts and offenses by putting a big, spiritual Band-Aid over their wounds. They sing a little louder in worship and jump a little higher in praise to try to suppress their hurt feelings. Yet a smiling face on the outside can't hide an offense festering on the inside for very long.

Additionally, pride often prevents people from admitting that they were hurt. They immediately put up walls and say, "Me, hurt? No, I'm not hurt." Pride causes big problems from the get-go! Humble yourself, don't worry about being vulnerable, and admit that you were hurt.

Release Your Offender

The second step is to take that hurt and lay it at the foot of the cross. Say, "Lord, I forgive that person for hurting me. I release him or her from everything he or she has done to hurt me. Lord, I choose to forgive that person. As You have forgiven me of my sins, Lord, I forgive that person for his or her sins against me. Amen."

When you humble yourself and pray this prayer of forgiveness, it will release you from the oppression unforgiveness puts on your heart. Once you forgive, you will feel as though the weight of the world has been removed from your shoulders. For a while, you may need to pray this prayer once or twice daily until the forgiveness is established in your heart.

Cast Out Negative Thoughts

The third step is to refuse to allow yourself to think negative thoughts about the person or people who hurt you.

> The weapons we fight with are not the weapons of the world. On the contrary, they have divine power to demolish strongholds. We demolish arguments and every pretension that sets itself up against the knowledge of God, and we take captive every thought to make it obedient to Christ. (2 Corinthians 10:4–5)

It's your responsibility to take every thought captive. Don't allow yourself to rehearse an offense. Don't allow yourself to think negative thoughts. If a negative thought about someone tries to slip in, begin speaking forth blessings over that person. Remember, your struggle is not against flesh and blood. (See Ephesians 6:12.) Your battle is not against the person who hurt you. Your battle is against the spiritual forces of evil in the heavenly realms. Don't lose the real battle by harboring unforgiveness in your heart and ungodly thoughts in your mind.

We need to stop focusing on the bad in people, even though it's usually obvious, and look instead with eyes of love for the good. I have said many times that before you get married, you see only the good in the person you are marrying, and after you get married, you see only the bad characteristics. This tendency does not promote forgiveness. True love never fails; it never fades out, becomes obsolete, or comes to an end. And it always forgives.

Pray for Your Offender

The fourth step is to pray for those who have hurt you. When you react out of your soul, you want to nurse and rehearse an offense. When you react out of your flesh, you want to punch the offender's lights out. But when you act out of your spirit, you pray for the person who has offended you, because that's what the Word tells you to do. Jesus said, *"Love your enemies and pray for those who persecute you"* (Matthew 5:44).

Pray that God would do for your enemies what you would want Him to do for you. Pray the blessings of God in their lives. Pray that the favor of God would be upon them. Don't allow your response to be based on the actions of others. Don't react; act out of your spirit and pray for those who have hurt you. Follow the instructions of Peter: *"Above all, love each other deeply, because love covers over a multitude of sins"* (1 Peter 4:8).

Express Forgiveness to Your Offender and Seek Reconciliation

The enemy loves to keep things in the dark, unexposed to the truth. It is crucial that we allow the evil deeds of darkness—the offenses—to be exposed under the light of God's truth. (See John 3:19–21.) Ask the Lord for wisdom on how to talk to and communicate openly with those who have offended you. Don't attack them, but communicate your feelings honestly and calmly. As you share openly, the evil deeds of darkness will be exposed under the light. Express forgiveness and seek reconciliation with those who have offended you. Then, you can continue living a victorious, fruitful life for the Lord.

> YOU CAN CONTINUE LIVING A VICTORIOUS, FRUITFUL LIFE FOR THE LORD.

After all, your reaction will determine your ultimate destiny—not only now, but also throughout eternity.

Chapter Fifteen: From the Pit of Unforgiveness to the Peak of Reconciliation

Points to Ponder

1. The Word of God says that we are to forgive others, just as our heavenly Father has forgiven us. (See Colossians 3:13.) According to Hebrews 12:14–15, what will spring up if we do not forgive?

2. Jesus said that we will experience offenses. How you react to offense determines your destiny. Give an example of how this has been true in your life.

3. The feeling of rejection, the refusal to forgive, and the unwillingness to admit that you've been hurt are often rooted in pride. Explain why this is so.

4. God wants us to practice "soul control." What is it, how do we practice it, and how can we make it a way of life?

5. List the five steps in the process of forgiveness, as outlined in this chapter.

Meditate on these Scriptures, speak them aloud, and commit them to memory.

If you forgive men when they sin against you, your heavenly Father will also forgive you. But if you do not forgive men their sins, your Father will not forgive your sins. (Matthew 6:14–15)

Bear with each other and forgive whatever grievances you may have against one another. Forgive as the Lord forgave you.
(Colossians 3:13)

Above all, love each other deeply, because love covers over a multitude of sins. (1 Peter 4:8)

Be kind and compassionate to one another, forgiving each other, just as in Christ God forgave you. (Ephesians 4:32)

—16—

From the Pit of Injustice to the Peak of Promotion

While my husband and I were separated prior to our divorce, he spread all kinds of untrue stories about me. The Lord told me not to defend myself, but instead to keep my mouth shut. After a year of my keeping silent, God opened the door for me to receive an hour of airtime on a large television network—and it was prime time! He spoke to my heart and said, "Because you have guarded your heart and your mouth and kept silent when I told you to, I can now trust you to bring forth my Word from your mouth." This was a confirmation of James 3:11–12: *"Can both fresh water and salt water flow from the same spring? My brothers, can a fig tree bear olives, or a grapevine bear figs? Neither can a salt spring produce fresh water."*

> **What Satan meant for evil, God will use for good.**

God wants to mature us. He wants to change us and heal us. He wants to get us to the place where we immediately release offenses when they come our way. The enemy tries to set us up for destruction when offense comes. But what Satan meant for evil, God will use for good. (See Genesis 50:20.)

God will set you up for promotion if you respond to offenses in a godly way. Promotion doesn't always look the way we thought it would look. In my personal experience, most of my promotions didn't even remotely resemble what I had envisioned. Promotion comes from the Lord, and it comes however He wants to bring it.

False Accusation Brings Promotion When We Keep Our Hearts Right

One of the most hurtful things is false accusation or slander spoken about us by others. One thing to keep in mind is that false accusations almost always precede supernatural promotion—*if* you keep your heart right and forgive your accusers. God uses false accusations as a platform for promotion if you pass the test and keep your heart right. Remember that Joseph was falsely accused by the wife of Potiphar, his master, but God was positioning him for promotion. (See Genesis 39:5–23; 41:1–44.)

There have been three major instances in my life when a false accusation against me supernaturally thrust me into the purposes of God. These accusations took me to the next level within a short amount of time because, by the grace of God, I kept my heart right.

A Minister Who Loses His Reputation Wins Souls

I know a young minister of the gospel who went through a devastating divorce. There were certain issues that he took full responsibility for, and he admitted his shortcomings. Yet the people in his community gossiped about him and, not knowing the whole story, even made up erroneous details to fill in the blanks. He repented, God restored him, and he went on to have a large, fruitful ministry. Everyone who had said that he could never be used by the Lord again served as a propelling force that actually encouraged him to grab hold of the forgiveness and unconditional love of God. He ended up going further in God and doing greater things than he had ever envisioned or imagined.

A Woman Surrenders to God and Reaps Unexpected Blessings

One of our evangelistic outreaches brought us to the door of a woman who said that she'd known Jesus at one time but wasn't ready to come back to Him. As a result of a false accusation, she had been fired from her job. Her phone service had been turned off because she couldn't afford to pay the bills, which meant that she could not be contacted by prospective employers to schedule interviews. In one week, her car was going to be repossessed, which would mean she wouldn't be able to get to the interviews anyway. To make matters worse, she had been refused unemployment benefits.

After we ministered to her, she struggled with the Lord, then finally surrendered and gave her life to Him. Within the week, someone anonymously paid her phone bill. Immediately, she received a call from a company where she had applied to work. After one interview, she got the job. And her unemployment benefits came through in an amount just large enough for her to pay the remainder of what she owed on her car. Talk about a promotion following false accusation!

When You Suffer Injustice or False Accusations...

Resist Seeking Revenge

When false accusations come our way, we should never try to take matters into our own hands, for doing so gives place to unforgiveness and bitterness, which could ultimately cost us our lives. God tells us, "*Vengeance is Mine; I will repay*" (Romans 12:19 NKJV). He makes it clear that He doesn't want us to try to get even or pay someone back for what that person did to us. And we're not to defend ourselves, either—that's God's job. "*Yet their Redeemer is strong; the Lord Almighty is his name. He will vigorously defend their cause so that he may bring rest to their land, but unrest to those who live in Babylon*" (Jeremiah 50:34).

When we try to defend ourselves, it's usually because of our pride. Pride is often a defense mechanism for insecurity. But when we know who we are in Christ, it doesn't matter what anyone thinks about us. All that matters is what God thinks.

Walk in Love

Just as we need to exercise our faith, we need to exercise our hearts by walking in love and forgiveness. It's easy to love people when everything is going our way. It's another thing to love people when we see their faults, and especially when their faults have hurt or wounded us.

Exercising our hearts to walk in love is a part of the process of becoming mature Christians. We can't do much for God if we allow the enemy to keep offense in our hearts. Even our prayers will be hindered. Realize that whenever we work or associate with other people, offenses will come; hurts will come. Again, it's how we handle those offenses that determines our destinies.

We grow in the tough times, not the easy ones. Don't try to escape hard, difficult times. Face them, embrace them, and grow through them. If you run away, you will hinder your growth. If you face them, you will become stronger and even more compassionate toward others. Some people get hurt and never get over it. It's your choice. Be determined to work all the way through offenses and keep exercising your heart to walk in love and forgiveness.

> *The LORD is compassionate and gracious, slow to anger, abounding in love.* (Psalm 103:8)

Just like our God, we are to be slow to anger and abounding in love. As 1 Corinthians 13 tells us, love is not touchy or fretful or resentful. Love keeps no record of wrongs, and it pays no attention to a suffered wrong. Love does not delight in evil or compromise but rejoices with the truth. Love does not rejoice at injustice and unrighteousness but rejoices when righteousness and truth prevail. Love always protects, always trusts, always hopes, and always perseveres—no matter what.

> *Love bears up under anything and everything that comes, is ever ready to believe the best of every person, its hopes are fadeless under all circumstances, and it endures everything [without weakening].* (1 Corinthians 13:7 AMP)

Remain Obedient

When we're waiting for a promotion that God told us would happen or for the fulfillment of promises that He gave us in His Word, we can be tempted to try to help Him out a little bit. When we do this, we get discouraged and frustrated because we are trying to take on a job that's way over our heads. We can end up making a mess of things, and sometimes, it takes even longer for God's plan to come about.

I knew what I was called to do from a young age, but in the midst of life's storms, I thought I should help God out a little bit. One day, the Lord said to me, "I don't need your help, just your obedience." When I withdrew my "help" and focused on taking one step of obedience at a time, things began to happen. It may not have been as fast as I would have liked, but things began to fall into place.

> *When Pharaoh let the people go, God did not lead them on the road through the Philistine country, though that was shorter. For God said, "If they face war, they might change their minds and return to Egypt." So God led the people around by the desert road toward the Red Sea. The Israelites went up out of Egypt armed for battle.*
>
> (Exodus 13:17–18)

When God ordained the Israelites' escape from Egypt, He thought the whole thing through and looked out for their best interests. He knew that the long way around would allow time for the work in them to be completed. He didn't want them to change their minds and return to their former bondage.

Maybe you feel like God has led you around and around by the desert road—the long route. I don't know about you, but I'm always looking for shortcuts when I drive. Yet that's the thing with God—we aren't allowed to drive. We must stay in the passenger seat and allow Him to be the driver. And the driver chooses the route. Whether He chooses the shortest route or the longest, He needs only our obedience. God does things the way He does because He wants all the glory.

> *The LORD said to Moses, "…And I will harden Pharaoh's heart, and he will pursue them. But I will gain glory for myself through Pharaoh and all his army, and the Egyptians will know that I am the LORD."*
>
> (Exodus 14:1, 4)

When God does things, everyone, including you, will know that He is God, and that your God has brought you forth.

WHEN GOD SAYS IT'S TIME, HE CAUSES EVERYTHING TO FALL INTO PLACE.

When God said it was time for me to start my television ministry, the doors swung open. I was a single mom who was standing in faith daily for diapers and baby food for my newborn daughter. But when God says it's time, He causes everything to fall into place. And, much to my own amazement, He didn't need any help from me—only my obedience every step of the way.

The Old Is Gone, the New Has Come

For you died, and your life is now hidden with Christ in God.
(Colossians 3:3)

We aren't the same old carnal, worldly people we used to be before accepting Christ. When we accepted Christ, we died—to sin, and to our old ways of dealing with and responding to things. As a matter of fact, dead people have no responses. Dead people don't even notice when bad things are done to them or when words are spoken against them—they're dead!

We are dead to our old selves and our former, sinful ways. We are new creations in Christ; we're no longer those creepy creatures filled with sin that we used to be.

Do not lie to each other, since you have taken off your old self with its practices and have put on the new self, which is being renewed in knowledge in the image of its Creator. (Colossians 3:9–10)

We must become what we already are in Christ. Colossians 3:12 instructs us, "*Therefore, as God's chosen people, holy and dearly loved, clothe yourselves with compassion, kindness, humility, gentleness and patience.*" We must choose to take off the old self and put on the new. No one gets you dressed in the morning, unless you are a small child or have a medical condition that makes you unable to dress yourself. When you are mature and healthy, you dress yourself. God's Word tells us what not to wear and what to put on. We shouldn't spend more time and attention on how we are dressed in the natural than we spend on how we are clothed in the spirit! Ask yourself, *Would I be voted the worst dressed or the best dressed when it comes to clothing myself in a way that pleases the Lord?*

The Lord is trying to get us dressed and ready for where we are going—a higher place in Him. This matters more than the injustices and false accusations we suffer. We need to put on the virtues listed in Colossians 3:12 and wear them all day long. I don't know about you, but for me, this verse is enough homework for a lifetime. And if we think we are already clothed with all of these attributes every day and don't need to work on them, pride is blocking the real picture.

And over all these virtues put on love, which binds them all together in perfect unity. (Colossians 3:14)

Most important, put on love. If we aren't clothed in love, there won't be any unity in our lives. Again, some people "put on" that they love. In other words, they act like they are walking in love. They act like they love you. They "put on" that they are in agreement with you. Then, when you turn your back, they talk about you without even realizing what they are doing. We cannot "put on" that we love people. We must make a decision to put on the genuine garment of love every day and stay clothed in love at all times.

Total Freedom

We experience total freedom in Christ only when we have allowed the Holy Spirit to fully remove any root of anger, bitterness, or unforgiveness from our hearts and lives. As we submit to this process, the Holy Spirit will do a complete work. It may take longer than you bargained for, it may hurt more than you ever imagined, but there will be blessings and promotion on the other side of your obedience. Our loving heavenly Father leads us on the path of forgiveness because He wants us to experience the abundant life that He has for us, both in this life and in the life to come. We must pursue total freedom in Christ through a lifestyle of forgiving and releasing others.

> OUR LOVING HEAVENLY FATHER LEADS US ON THE PATH OF FORGIVENESS BECAUSE HE WANTS US TO EXPERIENCE THE ABUNDANT LIFE THAT HE HAS FOR US.

When my former husband died, some of his family members threatened me, saying that if I attended his funeral, they would have me arrested on the spot. I was totally devastated and in pain at the time. It was not only my former husband who had died, but also the father of my child! I needed to grieve the loss that both my daughter and I had experienced.

I was not welcome at the viewing or the funeral service, so we arranged a private viewing for my daughter and me because Destiny wanted to give her dad one of her favorite stuffed animals. The funeral home allowed us in, and Destiny put the toy on top of her dad's heart. She said she wanted him to have it with him in heaven. At the time, my precious four-year-old was grieving a loss that she would have to live with for the rest of her life. I was grieving, too, and yet I had to acknowledge the pain that my former husband's family members were dealing with and choose to walk free from any unforgiveness and bitterness.

My family came to town to attend the funeral service with me. In order to attend the service, my father had even received special permission to suspend a treatment he was undergoing at the hospital for a heart condition. Yet, upon our arrival, we were met at the door and asked to leave. Angry individuals confronted me as I entered the funeral service, and I was told that a police sergeant would be over momentarily to arrest me if I didn't leave immediately. Clinging to my father's arm, I prayed that the stress of the situation would not cause him to have another heart attack as I waited for the sergeant to arrive.

I tried to comfort my dad by saying, "Don't worry, Dad. They falsely accused Jesus, too."

As I said those words, it was as though I heard angels singing, and I saw a vision of Jesus carrying His cross up the hill of Golgotha. I experienced the presence and peace of the Lord very powerfully that day.

No one ever showed up to arrest me. The threatening comments had been an attempt to intimidate me into leaving. We stayed, we grieved, and my parents all but carried me out to the car at the end of the service. Once again, I was faced with the choice to forgive. And again, to do this, I needed to acknowledge the pain that his family members were facing at that time, as well. Because I forgave them, I was blessed with the ability to move forward.

A couple of days before my former husband's death, I had been in a time of fasting and prayer when the Lord clearly spoke to me from this Scripture:

Enlarge the place of your tent, stretch your tent curtains wide, do not hold back; lengthen your cords, strengthen your stakes. For you will spread out to the right and to the left; your descendants will dispossess nations and settle in their desolate cities. Do not be afraid; you will not suffer shame. Do not fear disgrace; you will not be humiliated. You will forget the shame of your youth and remember no more the reproach of your widowhood. For your Maker is your husband—the LORD Almighty is his name. (Isaiah 54:2–5)

I was encouraged to know that growth was coming for my ministry. God was also saying that the day would come when everything that I had been through would seem as though it was from another life. I didn't have full understanding of what He was saying until a few days later. With the verse *"You will...remember no more the reproach of your widowhood,"* God had been preparing me for an unexpected *suddenly*—the death of Destiny's dad. The reproach that I went through during the funeral was deeply painful, yet God had said, *"You will...remember no more the reproach of your widowhood."*

Forgiving Yourself

Many of the people to whom I have had the privilege of ministering over the years have needed to forgive themselves for mistakes they have made and for perceived mistakes they have made. I say "perceived mistakes" because I have seen many people label choices "mistakes," when I don't believe that's how the Lord would label them.

We all make choices and decisions out of our brokenness and out of where we are in life. Disobedience is one thing, but making a decision out of your brokenness is another. When God tells you to do or not to do something and you blatantly disobey His instruction, that is disobedience. Disobedience to God is sin, so repent and make things right before the Lord. Then, forgive yourself and "grow" forward.

But don't label something "disobedience" or a "mistake" if, in reality, you were doing your best to make a choice or a decision to follow God's will for your life. You simply made a decision by looking through the lens of your own brokenness. When the child of an alcoholic grows up and marries an alcoholic, she most likely made her decision as she looked through the rose-colored glasses of her own brokenness and need.

As you grow forward in a life of wholeness through Christ, don't continually beat yourself up over choices you've made that don't seem wise today. You aren't the same person today you were then. You have grown and developed a life of wholeness through Christ. Do you know why hindsight is always twenty-twenty? Because all of us "grow forward" in life. So, stop being so hard on yourself.

Chapter Sixteen: From the Pit of Injustice to the Peak of Promotion

Points to Ponder

1. Have you ever been slandered or falsely accused? If so, how did it make you feel? How did you respond?

2. What should we resist doing when we suffer injustice or false accusations?

3. What does the test of injustice reveal about the heart?

4. Why does passing this test lead to promotion?

5. In order for us to experience total freedom in Christ in the area of injustice, what must we do?

Meditate on these Scriptures, speak them aloud, and commit them to memory.

Do not take revenge, my friends, but leave room for God's wrath, for it is written: "It is mine to avenge; I will repay," says the Lord.
(Romans 12:19)

Therefore, as God's chosen people, holy and dearly loved, clothe yourselves with compassion, kindness, humility, gentleness and patience. Bear with each other and forgive whatever grievances you may have against one another. Forgive as the Lord forgave you.
(Colossians 3:12–13)

[Love]…keeps no record of wrongs.…It always protects, always trusts, always hopes, always perseveres. Love never fails.
(1 Corinthians 13:5, 7–8)

Set your minds on things above, not on earthly things. For you died, and your life is now hidden with Christ in God. (Colossians 3:2–3)

—17—

KEY CHOICES TO
GET OUT OF ANY PIT

Every day of our lives, we make hundreds of choices. Those choices always produce either increase or decease in various areas of life. For example, when I decide to get up early and exercise, I make a choice that increases my health, even though it may decrease the amount of sleep that I get. Stop and think about it. Every decision creates increase or decrease. We must be led by the Holy Spirit and choose wisely. Our choices usually determine how long we stay in the pit, so choose wisely and get out of there!

Key Choice: Act, Don't React

A good example of acting rather than reacting is found in the twentieth chapter of 2 Chronicles. As we discussed earlier, Jehoshaphat, the king of Judah, heard from some of his men that a vast army was coming against him, and that they weren't far away. They weren't just an army; they were a vast army—a really, really, really big army! And they were not only coming after Jehoshaphat; they were also coming to destroy the whole city and everyone in it. What's more, they were advancing quickly. (See 2 Chronicles 20:1–2.)

It's one thing when a storm or a battle is coming, but it's a whole different thing when that storm is the size of Texas! The Word tells us that Jehoshaphat was alarmed, yet he did not react out of his flesh. Rather, he acted out of his spirit, meaning he took a deep breath and went to God with his troubles. (See verses 3–12.)

When we react out of our flesh, we freak out. We cry, we scream, we yell, we emit other unproductive responses. Some people even run away from God at the very time when they need to run *to* God the most. Yet, again, Jehoshaphat didn't react out of his flesh; he acted out of his spirit. Verse three tells us, *"Jehoshaphat resolved to inquire of the LORD, and he proclaimed a fast for all Judah."* And in verse four, we read, *"The people of Judah came together to seek help from the LORD."* In the midst of the biggest battle or storm of Jehoshaphat's life, he inquired of the Lord. He didn't inquire of his friends, his pastor, his boss, or his spouse. He came before the Lord in fasting and prayer, and he encouraged those around him to do the same.

Key Choice: Don't Panic in the Pit

When we panic in the pit, we often grab hold of anything we can get our hands on—anything that we think might keep us from going deeper into the pit. Actually, the opposite usually proves true. If we panic in the pit, the thing we grab on to actually serves as a shovel and takes us deeper.

You've probably seen this before—a person who grabs on to, for example, a new relationship in an attempt to get out of a relational pit. What happens? Instead of getting out of that previous relational pit, he winds up going even deeper into it. Or, perhaps you know someone who grabbed a drug or a drink in an attempt to numb the pain from his pit, only to find himself in a deeper, darker, even more painful pit. Don't panic in the pit. Again, the key is not to *react* out of your flesh, or your carnal instincts, but to *act* out of your spirit!

Jehoshaphat was alarmed when he learned that a vast army much larger than his was coming to make war with him. He was alarmed, but he did not panic. He did not react. He acted. Many times, we react emotionally to our pits or to the crises at hand. As a result, we waste all our time and energy, and we don't help the situations at all. As a matter of fact, we may even make things worse.

After waiting many, many years to get married, I found myself in an abusive marriage to a man who, as I've shared, had a sexual addiction. After dating for a year, we got married, and I immediately saw a side of him that he had never allowed me to see.

It took me a few years to realize that my husband had a sexual addiction, but as soon as I did, I panicked in the pit! I didn't act out of my spirit by any stretch of the imagination. I reacted out of my flesh with a full-blown panic attack in the pit.

When we find ourselves at the edge of a deep, dark pit, reacting out of our flesh is the worst thing we can do. When we react, we operate out of our sinful natures, our emotions, or our natural minds. Reacting to the pit or the battle you are up against acknowledges how big and how powerful the enemy is. But when we act out of our spirits, we acknowledge how much bigger and how much more powerful *God* is. This enables us to successfully come out of every pit that dares to entrap us.

Unlike me, Jehoshaphat acted. Jehoshaphat proclaimed a fast so that he might hear from God on how to handle the situation at hand. Not only did Jehoshaphat seek the Lord, but he also proclaimed a fast for all Judah. Everyone in the surrounding towns came together to fast and to seek God's direction. The people responded according to how Jehoshaphat handled the situation. If Jehoshaphat had panicked and had come unglued, the people around him would have done the same thing. When we react out of our emotions rather than act out of our spirits, we give place for the enemy to defeat us. But, if we act out of our spirits, if we look to the Lord for how to handle the situations we face, then we always come out on the winning side.

> IF WE LOOK TO THE LORD FOR HOW TO HANDLE THE SITUATIONS WE FACE, THEN WE ALWAYS COME OUT ON THE WINNING SIDE.

When we panic, we try to do in the flesh what can be done only in the spirit. Again, when we get in the flesh, we can dig an even deeper pit. It is my desire that you will refuse to grab a shovel but grab the rope of hope instead and determine to climb out, no matter how deep your pit may seem today.

Key Choice: Determine to Trust God

"Jehoshaphat resolved to inquire of the LORD*"* (2 Chronicles 20:3, emphasis added). *To resolve* essentially means the same thing as *to determine.* So, as we discussed, Jehoshaphat determined to inquire of the Lord—not

his friends, not his coworkers, not his family, but the Lord! And think about Joseph. That young man was totally alone in his pit, without a friend or brother in sight. So, whether we are alone in the pit or sitting there with the opinionated words of others swirling about our heads, our first and best option is to inquire of the Lord and get *His* opinion on things.

When the people of Judah all gathered at the temple, Jehoshaphat stood up and prayed. He started his prayer by acknowledging God as the all-powerful, all-knowing One, saying, *"Power and might are in your hand, and no one can withstand you"* (2 Chronicles 20:6). When we acknowledge God for who He is, we don't have any trouble letting Him be in control. But when we forget what He's done for us in the past and doubt what He will do for us in the future, we start acting out of our own strength; we want to take control ourselves.

Jehoshaphat acknowledged God in his situation. As a result, he looked to God for the solution to the problem. The Bible instructs us, *"Trust in the LORD with all your heart and lean not on your own understanding; in all your ways acknowledge him, and he will make your paths straight"* (Proverbs 3:5–6). We need to recognize and acknowledge who God is in the midst of our pits and battles. Again, sometimes, we can get so caught up in acknowledging how big the opposing army is or how deep our pit is that we get distracted and forget that God is bigger and is still in control.

Jehoshaphat was determined to inquire of the Lord. Determination will get us just about anywhere we want to go. If we are determined to go in a direction that's the opposite of God's direction for our lives, we can. It won't be pretty, and it won't be fun, but our determination can take us in that direction—at least for a little while.

If we are determined not to quit, we can successfully make it out of whatever pit we find ourselves in. As a young Christian, I felt as though I didn't have any gifts that I could use to bring glory to God. I told God, "I can't sing, I can't play the piano...God, I don't have any gifts." It was years later when the Lord said to me, "Danette, your gift is the gift of determination."

Well, I had never considered determination a gift. But all of us have gifts that we don't even realize. God gives us whatever gifts we need to

> GOD GIVES US WHATEVER GIFTS WE NEED TO FULFILL HIS CALL AND PURPOSE FOR OUR LIVES.

fulfill His call and purpose for our lives. As I look back over my life, I can definitely say that God gave me the gift I needed the most—the gift of determination.

However, determination can work to our disadvantage if we are determined to go against God.

Have you ever heard someone comment, "Today was a Jonah day"? When someone says that, you know he means that he's had a very hard day or experienced an above-average rough time! Well, let's look at how rough it got for Jonah in his misguided determination.

The Lord directed him to Nineveh, where he was to convict the people of their wickedness. But Jonah was determined to go to Tarshish instead— and that's exactly where he set out to go! His trip didn't last long, and it wasn't pretty, but that's the direction in which his determination took him.

The word of the LORD came to Jonah son of Amittai: "Go to the great city of Nineveh and preach against it, because its wickedness has come up before me." But Jonah ran away from the LORD and headed for Tarshish. He went down to Joppa, where he found a ship bound for that port. After paying the fare, he went aboard and sailed for Tarshish to flee from the LORD. (Jonah 1:1–3)

Jonah paid the fare to go in the opposite direction from the Word of the Lord. At the time, the fare seemed cheap, but the fare for disobedience is always extremely expensive. Sometimes, it can cost us everything, including our lives.

Because of God's great love, He sent a violent storm to give Jonah another opportunity to use his determination to take him in the right direction. The storm was so violent that the ship on which Jonah was traveling threatened to break up. As the seas became rougher and rougher, Jonah admitted to everyone on the ship that they were going through the storm as a result of *his* disobedience.

Earlier, we saw that storms can come into our lives as a result of our disobedience, other people's disobedience, or directly from the hand of God to prune us and to cause us to be even more fruitful. Jonah is an excellent example of this truth. When we walk in disobedience, God often allows storms to come into our lives to get us back on track. He not only allows storms to get our attention, but He also supernaturally provides a way out of the storms.

After Jonah confessed his responsibility for the storm, he directed the sailors to throw him overboard. So, *"they took Jonah and threw him overboard, and the raging sea grew calm....But the* LORD *provided a great fish to swallow Jonah, and Jonah was inside the fish three days and three nights"* (Jonah 1:15, 17). After the storm subsided, Jonah woke up in the whale's stomach with his head in a tangle of seaweed. Now, that's a pit! What was the first thing Jonah did when he realized his predicament? He prayed.

Key Choice: Pray in the Pit

Always pray in the pit! If you aren't sure how to pray, you can borrow a few words from Jonah:

From inside the fish Jonah prayed to the LORD *his God. He said: "In my distress I called to the* LORD, *and he answered me. From the depths of the grave I called for help, and you listened to my cry. You hurled me into the deep, into the very heart of the seas, and the currents swirled about me; all your waves and breakers swept over me. I said, 'I have been banished from your sight; yet I will look again toward your holy temple.' The engulfing waters threatened me, the deep surrounded me; seaweed was wrapped around my head. To the roots of the mountains I sank down; the earth beneath barred me in forever. But you brought my life up from the pit, O* LORD *my God. When my life was ebbing away, I remembered you,* LORD, *and my prayer rose to you, to your holy temple. Those who cling to worthless idols forfeit the grace that could be theirs. But I, with a song of thanksgiving, will sacrifice to you. What I have vowed I will make good. Salvation comes from the* LORD."

(Jonah 2:1–9)

Immediately after praying, Jonah was delivered from his pit. *"The* LORD *commanded the fish, and it vomited Jonah onto dry land"* (Jonah 2:10). God repeated His command for Jonah to preach His message to the people of Nineveh, and this time, he obeyed. (See Jonah 3:1–3.)

> **THE LORD BROUGHT JONAH UP OUT OF THE PIT, AND HE WILL DO THE SAME FOR YOU TODAY.**

There's nothing like a pit to get you to pray. Some of the best prayer times that I have ever had have been while I was in a pit! Don't quit in the pit, but pray like you have never prayed before.

The Lord brought Jonah up out of the pit, and He will do the same for you today. It doesn't matter how or why you got in the pit. The important thing is that you don't quit in the pit, but that you grab hold of the rope of hope and climb out.

Key Choice: Don't Dwell on Your Circumstances

No matter what storms come our way, we must be determined to look up, get up, and never give up. When we look up, we are looking unto the Lord. Don't look down in discouragement, and don't look around you at the overwhelming circumstances; look up to the Lord. As we look to the Lord, He gives us the strength to get up. He actually carries us and holds us up during our times of need. If we always look up and choose to get up, we are well on our way to never giving up.

> *But Jonah ran away from the LORD and headed for Tarshish. He went down to Joppa, where he found a ship bound for that port. After paying the fare, he went aboard and sailed for Tarshish to flee from the LORD.*
> (Jonah 1:3)

As we discussed earlier, Jonah made a bad choice, which ended up costing him a great price. Disobedience always ends up costing a higher price than you ever could have imagined. Jonah's disobedience affected everyone else on the ship bound for Tarshish. They, too, had to weather *his* storm. When other people in our lives walk in disobedience, we can be affected by their storms. After all, we're in the boat with them.

> *Then the LORD sent a great wind on the sea, and such a violent storm arose that the ship threatened to break up.* (Jonah 1:4)

God sent a storm in order to get Jonah back in the bounds of His will. Sometimes, we find ourselves in situations where our ships (our lives) are threatening to break into a million pieces because Father is trying to get us back on track.

Jonah was given a second chance to make a choice, and that time, he made the right one. He chose to get up out of his mess. Look again at what Jonah told the people who were with him:

> *"Pick me up and throw me into the sea,"* he replied, *"and it will become calm. I know that it is my fault that this great storm has come upon you."*   (Jonah 1:12)

In other words, Jonah said, "Help me get up out of my mess." He owned the responsibility for the storm. He didn't shift the blame. He didn't search for a scapegoat. He acknowledged his disobedience, and he was determined to focus forward.

> *But the LORD provided a great fish to swallow Jonah, and Jonah was inside the fish three days and three nights.*   (Jonah 1:17)

The Lord made provision for Jonah when he decided to get up out of his mess. God provided, even in the middle of the raging ocean in the midst of a scary storm. God will always make miraculous provision for us when we make the choice to get up out of our messes. No matter what your mess is today, and no matter how you got there, when you make the choice to get up out of your mess, Father will hold your hand and gently lead you out—one step at a time.

Key Choice: Focus on the Finish Line

Another key I've learned about how to succeed in getting to the other side of my storms is focusing forward, or focusing on the finish line. The Lord is so awesome in that He allows us to see the finish line before the race even starts. He shows us the finish line first so we'll be encouraged never to quit or give up in the midst of the race.

If we never quit or give up, we can never be defeated. We will always win. But at the starting line, you have no idea what you will face in the upcoming race. You know only about the finish line—the place where God showed you that you would be going. If we remain focused on the finish line, we won't fall for the distractions and discouragement that we encounter in the midst of the race.

I'm amazed when I see people who jog every morning—rain, snow, sleet, or shine. They aren't deterred by the weather. They have a goal, and they don't allow storms to stop them.

I consider my life worth nothing to me, if only I may finish the race and complete the task the Lord Jesus has given me—the task of testifying to the gospel of God's grace.   (Acts 20:24)

Our goal in life needs to be to do everything the Lord has created us to do and to finish the race. He wants to show us the finish line, which is the fulfillment of our purpose and call in life. The sooner we learn about our finish line, the better.

Yes, the Lord reveals things in different seasons of our lives. We may not know every detail of the picture, but we can have a general framework that leads us in the right direction. It's important that we are on the right track as we are running the race. Then, when distractions and discouragement come our way, we can press past them and remain focused on the finish line.

God revealed to Joseph his purpose—his finish line—through a dream when Joseph was young. (See Genesis 37:5–9.) God made the finish line very clear to him. He didn't have to question or guess what God wanted him to do. Joseph had seen his finish line clearly before even starting the race. And it was a good thing, too, because Joseph would go through many storms; he had many opportunities to quit before he actually reached the finish line.

As soon as Joseph saw his finish line and started the race, the opposition began. The dream that the Lord had given him hadn't revealed all the twists and turns that the race would entail. The glorious dream hadn't included the pit or the prison. Joseph was shown only the palace—the finish line. Although the dream hadn't included the details of challenges and trials, Joseph still had to go from the pit to the prison on his way to the palace. And the thing I love about Joseph is, he didn't quit in the pit!

As we discussed, the most painful part of the pit was that Joseph's own brothers were the ones who put him there.

If an enemy were insulting me, I could endure it; if a foe were raising
himself against me, I could hide from him. But it is you, a man like
myself, my companion, my close friend, with whom I once enjoyed
sweet fellowship as we walked with the throng at the house of God.

(Psalm 55:12–14)

The hardest hurts to endure are the ones that come from those closest
to us. Yet Joseph maintained a right heart attitude through his entire or-
deal. Joseph kept his heart right, he served God with all of his heart in spite
of his circumstances, and he kept dreaming about the finish line.

After Joseph's brothers had thrown him in the pit and plotted his
death, they decided to change their strategy. They began to reason that
there had to be a more profitable way to dispose of Joseph than leaving him
to die—a way that would bring them even greater rewards. They decided
that selling him into slavery would be more advantageous to them. So,
they conspired against their brother and sold him to a group of merchants
headed to Egypt, then lied to their father by claiming Joseph was dead.
(See Genesis 37:26–33.)

What the brothers failed to realize was that Joseph was destined for
the palace. He had already seen the finish line, and he wasn't about to quit,
no matter what pits trapped him along the way.

The LORD was with Joseph and he prospered, and he lived in the house
of his Egyptian master. When his master saw that the LORD was with
him and that the LORD gave him success in everything he did, Joseph
found favor in his eyes and became his attendant. Potiphar put him
in charge of his household, and he entrusted to his care everything he
owned. (Genesis 39:2–4)

Even when Joseph was sold into slavery, he ultimately prospered and
had success because the Lord was with him. We must remember that even
the heart of the king is in the hand of the Lord. (See Proverbs 21:1.) Joseph
remained focused on the finish line and not on the wrongs that his brothers had done to him. As a result, he was not derailed from his course.

Joseph was later thrown into prison, although he was innocent of any
wrongdoing. He was stripped of his position of privilege as a result of false

accusations. Yet God was strategically positioning him for his place in the palace. Remember, false accusations almost *always* precede supernatural promotion!

> *So Pharaoh sent for Joseph, and he was quickly brought from the dungeon. When he had shaved and changed his clothes, he came before Pharaoh.* (Genesis 41:14)

At God's appointed time, Joseph was ready to cross that finish line because he had maintained a right heart attitude and a godly character. Character really does count, and, like Joseph, we find that character is what keeps us running the race successfully, all the way to the finish line.

During the course of the race of life, we are prepared by God for what awaits us at the finish line—the fulfillment of our purpose. We grow in wisdom, discernment, and character before crossing the finish line.

> *Then Pharaoh said to Joseph, "Since God has made all this known to you, there is no one so discerning and wise as you. You shall be in charge of my palace, and all my people are to submit to your orders. Only with respect to the throne will I be greater than you."* (Genesis 41:39–40)

After Joseph interpreted Pharaoh's dream, he saw the fulfillment of his own dream. Everything that God had showed him and told him came to pass, though many years later. Everything that God has showed you and told you will come to pass, too, if you *don't quit in the pit.* Just keep focusing on the finish line. The pit isn't permanent—it's just a temporary pit stop on your path to the palace.

Key Choice: Don't Quit in the Pit

Like Joseph, I knew where I was going at a young age. However, I had many unexpected circumstances come my way. The last thing I ever expected to be was a single mom. I had started in the ministry at age nineteen, and I had served God all of my adult life. All of a sudden, the unexpected storm of divorce and single parenthood threw me in a pit, and boy, did I want to quit! Not only did I feel like quitting, but there were also people around me who told me my ministry was over. Hearing that was like being in the bottom of the pit and watching everyone around me shovel dirt on top of my head in an attempt to kill me.

God kept telling me to focus on the finish line. He used the life of Joseph to encourage me, and He told me to keep my heart right and my mouth shut. Father kept reassuring me that nothing could disqualify me from my call in Him—except my own choices. No one else's choices could disqualify me, not even my former husband's. As long as I chose to keep my heart free from unforgiveness and bitterness, and as long as I chose to be obedient and do daily what the Lord was leading me to do, He said, "Everything's going to be all right."

I want to encourage you today: Never quit! The only thing that can disqualify you is your heart attitude and your choices. And as long as you choose to obey the Holy Spirit's leading—even when you receive seemingly illogical instructions—you will come into all the blessings that the Lord has for you. Your call hasn't changed. God's purpose for your life hasn't changed. Your address may have changed, your income may have changed, your circumstances may have changed, but your God never changes. He's the same yesterday, today, and forever. (See Hebrews 13:8.) He's still on the throne, and Jesus is sitting at the right hand of the Father, interceding for you and me. (See Romans 8:34.)

> GOD IS STILL ON THE THRONE, AND JESUS IS SITTING AT THE RIGHT HAND OF THE FATHER, INTERCEDING FOR YOU AND ME.

Maybe you have never sought God concerning His purpose for your life. Maybe you have never accepted Him into your life as your Savior. Again, today can be your day to do so! Don't wait to be thrown into a pit before seeking God. If, however, you are in a pit today, there's no better place to call on the name of the Lord. He's just waiting for you to call on His name. First, you look up to the Lord; then, you choose daily to get up and pursue the finish line.

Chapter Seventeen: Key Choices to Get Out of Any Pit

Points to Ponder

1. Think of a difficult situation that you are facing or have faced and list ways that you acted, not reacted, in response to it.

2. Why are the choices we make so important in the process of getting out of our pits?

3. List the seven key choices outlined in this chapter.

4. Which one of these choices is the hardest for you to make and act on? Why?

5. What will focusing on the finish line do for you in the midst of a storm? What will it prevent you from doing?

Meditate on these Scriptures, speak them aloud, and commit them to memory.

Trust in the Lord *with all your heart and lean not on your own understanding; in all your ways acknowledge him, and he will make your paths straight.* (Proverbs 3:5–6)

Commit to the Lord *whatever you do, and your plans will succeed.* (Proverbs 16:3)

I sought the Lord, *and he answered me; he delivered me from all my fears.* (Psalm 34:4)

Let us fix our eyes on Jesus, the author and perfecter of our faith, who for the joy set before him endured the cross, scorning its shame, and sat down at the right hand of the throne of God. Consider him who endured such opposition from sinful men, so that you will not grow weary and lose heart. (Hebrews 12:2–3)

—18—

Climbing to the Next Level

O nce God has gotten you out of your pit, the journey is far from over. When you're out of the pit—and, sometimes, even when you're still in the pit—God will use you to help others out of their pits, too. This chapter is about preparing to see others through their storms.

Rebuilding the Walls

In the book of Nehemiah, the title character requested a leave of absence to go on a trip to help those in need by rebuilding the wall around Jerusalem. The Israelites were in a pit of despair because their beloved city was in ruins. Because Nehemiah had a heart for the people, the king was pleased to send him.

> *The king asked me, "Why does your face look so sad when you are not ill? This can be nothing but sadness of heart." I was very much afraid, but I said to the king, "May the king live forever! Why should my face not look sad when the city where my fathers are buried lies in ruins, and its gates have been destroyed by fire?"...I answered the king, "If it pleases the king and if your servant has found favor in his sight, let him send me to the city in Judah where my fathers are buried so that I can rebuild it."...It pleased the king to send me; so I set a time.*
>
> (Nehemiah 2:2–3, 5–6)

When God rebuilds the walls that have been broken down in your life and repairs the areas of brokenness you experience, He wants to use you to help rebuild the broken walls in the lives of other people. You can free others from their pits and, like Nehemiah, restore the ruins of their lives, thereby enabling them to enjoy the abundant life that God has for them and possess all His promises of blessing.

Have a Heart for the People

Nehemiah had a heart for his people because he was moved with the same desire to see the wall of Jerusalem restored. When something hits home with us or we have experienced it ourselves, we can easily have hearts of compassion for other people who are dealing with the same thing. Most of my greatest teachings have come as a result of the things I have been through. It's one thing to preach the Word, and it's a whole different thing to preach the Word of God that you have experienced to be true in your own life. When this happens, you minister the Word with an anointing and a passion that prove to be life-changing and faith-building for others.

People usually need to know that we have a heart for them—that we feel their pain, that we've been in their shoes—before they will allow us to help them rebuild the broken-down walls in their lives.

Call upon God's Equipping

I also said to him, "If it pleases the king, may I have letters to the governors of Trans-Euphrates, so that they will provide me safe-conduct until I arrive in Judah? And may I have a letter to Asaph, keeper of the king's forest, so he will give me timber to make beams for the gates of the citadel by the temple and for the city wall and for the residence I will occupy?" And because the gracious hand of my God was upon me, the king granted my requests. (Nehemiah 2:7–8)

When Nehemiah requested letters of reference, the king not only granted his request, but he also gave Nehemiah even more than he asked for. Because the hand of God was upon Nehemiah, the king granted his requests—and then some! When you have the favor of God, you can't help

WHEN YOU HAVE THE FAVOR OF GOD, YOU CAN'T HELP BUT HAVE THE FAVOR OF MAN.

but have the favor of man. Remember, even the hearts of the kings are in the hand of the Lord. (See Proverbs 21:1.)

It always pleases the Lord when you have a heart for His people; if you love them, He will send you to help them rebuild their lives. And when the King of Kings sends you, you will have everything you need.

> *So the wall was completed...in fifty-two days. When all our enemies heard about this, all the surrounding nations were afraid and lost their self-confidence, because they realized that this work had been done with the help of our God.* (Nehemiah 6:15–16)

Be Available and Ready

Nehemiah is a good example for us to follow. He made himself available to be used by God. He had a heart of compassion for the people, he encouraged them, and, together, they rebuilt the wall—and their lives—with help from the hand of God. The Lord wants this to be a part of each of our testimonies. He wants us to say that we help others rebuild their lives for the glory of God.

God will get the glory out of every pit in which we find ourselves—if we keep our hearts right, continually focus forward, and remain available for the Lord's use. The Word says that *"many are called, but few are chosen"* (Matthew 22:14 NKJV). I believe the reason for this is that, along the way, many people lose their availability and cannot be chosen. When we submit to the Lord's rebuilding process in our lives and reach out to help others rebuild, the enemy doesn't take it sitting down. Satan will try to stir things up, just as he did with Nehemiah.

> *When Sanballat the Horonite and Tobiah the Ammonite official heard about* [the plans to rebuild the wall], *they were very much disturbed that someone had come to promote the welfare of the Israelites.* (Nehemiah 2:10)

Just as Nehemiah's enemies were not happy about his plans to rebuild the wall and tried to distract him from his work (see Nehemiah 6:1–3), the enemy likes to get us so caught up in our own lives that we don't have the time or energy to reach out and help others rebuild their own walls. That's why it's important to get our eyes off of ourselves. If we keep our eyes on the Lord and maintain hearts of compassion for others, we will remain available for kingdom purposes. After all, no matter how badly we are hurting, no matter how much we have been through, there is always someone hurting worse than we are. There's always someone who has been through more than we have.

I'm not saying you should deny your pain or forgo a time of healing for yourself. But I am saying, don't camp out there. Get up out of your own mess and go seed your need by reaching out to someone who is hurting even more than you are. This type of availability immediately cancels any pity parties that you may be tempted to throw.

What I call the availability test is a hard one. I've wanted to throw in the towel many times and get a well-paying job that uses my education and talents. But if we are willing to give up everything for the Lord, we will always come out on top, and we can help others to get there, too.

When I travel with Destiny, she often misses birthday parties and special events at school and church. Many times, we are out of town—or even out of the country—at the same time when a big event is planned. Sometimes, Grandma comes to stay with her, but when I know that the Lord wants her along on a trip, I take her with me. My answer to her is the same answer the Lord has given me since I was nineteen years old: To whom much is given, much is required. (See Luke 12:48 NKJV.) Although she may leave town with some disappointment in her heart, she always returns with great joy. God always gives her something better when she travels according to His will than what she missed back home—every time! When we stay available to God, His will always takes us to places of great satisfaction and joy—always.

If we stay available, there is no limit to what God can and will do through us. Not only do we need to stay available to the Lord for His use, but we must also stay ready. You can be available but not ready. You are ready when you have prepared yourself.

THERE IS NO LIMIT TO WHAT GOD CAN AND WILL DO THROUGH US.

If I had not stayed available to God during the storms in my life, I wouldn't be writing this book today. Also, I would have missed out on the joy and satisfaction of years spent ministering to millions through television and multiple thousands through other various outreaches. If you realize today that you failed the availability test somewhere along the way, don't worry—there's no limit as to how many times you can retake it. Get on your face before the Lord and cry out, "Here I am, Lord. Use me."

Persevere Patiently during the Process

Once I passed the availability test, I advanced to the process of getting ready to cross over to the next level, both in my relationship with the Lord and in my ministry. After making up my mind that, no matter what came my way, I was going to stay available to the Lord, I wanted to get the show on the road. I was ready for things to start happening for me and my ministry. I was finally focusing forward, but I was in a hurry. I was looking for the fast-forward button but couldn't find it.

One day, the Lord said to me, "Relax. You're in process."

Relaxing has never been a natural thing for me; I live life in fifth gear most of the time. So, to hear that I had to relax in the midst of the "process" didn't set too well with me. I came to find out that the process took time and was painful. I was going to have to deal with trials of many kinds—so many kinds that they wouldn't all fit in this book.

What is "process," exactly? Again, often, it is facing trials of many kinds.

> Consider it pure joy, my brothers, whenever you face trials of many kinds, because you know that the testing of your faith develops perseverance. Perseverance must finish its work so that you may be mature and complete, not lacking anything.   (James 1:2–4)

The Word says that perseverance "*must finish its work.*" There's no way around it. There are no shortcuts in the things of God. Only after perseverance finishes its work in our lives will we be mature and complete. *To persevere* means "to persist in a state, enterprise, or undertaking in spite of counterinfluences, opposition, or discouragement." If we persevere, we never quit or give up.

If we aren't mature and complete through the working of perseverance in our trials, we will lack in many areas and be of little help to others. But when perseverance has finished its work, we will not lack anything. At that point, we will not only be available but also ready to be used by the Lord in a big way!

Webster's New World College Dictionary defines *process* as "the course of being done;…a continuing development involving many changes; a particular method of doing something, generally involving a number of steps or operations," as well as "to prepare by or subject to a special process or method."

Why must we go through the process? Because it's the process that makes us who God wants us to be—mature and complete believers. The process builds our characters and humbles us; in other words, it's less of self and more of God in our lives. Relax and enjoy the process.

Don't Doubt Your Abilities or Resources

Throughout the Bible, God just about always did big things with small resources. He rarely did big things with big resources.

Taking the five loaves and the two fish and looking up to heaven, [Jesus] gave thanks and broke the loaves. Then he gave them to the disciples, and the disciples gave them to the people. They all ate and were satisfied, and the disciples picked up twelve basketfuls of broken pieces that were left over. The number of those who ate was about five thousand men, besides women and children. (Matthew 14:19–21)

In the feeding of the five thousand, Jesus first took what He had, but that's where most people quit. They look at their resources and get depressed and discouraged, feel sorry for themselves, or try to manipulate others to give them resources. Simply use what you have, then trust the Lord.

Second, Jesus looked up to heaven. Don't look down; look up and hold your head up. This is where your faith and trust come in.

Third, Jesus gave thanks. Thank God for what you have. Stop complaining about what you don't have and start praising God for what you do have. A grateful, thankful heart is always a forerunner for an increase in blessing. If you aren't thankful for what you have, why would God give you more?

Fourth and finally, Jesus took a step of faith. Although He had only five loaves of bread and two fish, He started giving out what He had—now, that was a step of faith! When we take a step of faith and just start doing what we know we should do, provision will always be there.

Everyone ate—all five thousand men—and that's not counting the women and children who were there! Not only did they all eat, but they were all satisfied, too. They didn't just get an appetizer. No one left hungry. They were all satisfied, and, on top of that, there were twelve basketfuls of food left over. Now, don't tell me that God doesn't do big things with small resources. Again, He rarely does big things with big resources, but He always does big things with small resources.

When we remain obedient to God's guidance, He will always give us what we need to accomplish what He wants us to accomplish—always! Yet, often, people don't do great things for God because they keep looking at what they don't have.

"We don't have the money." Well, God owns it all.

"We don't have the workers we need." Well, you and God are the majority, so don't let a lack of workers be a cop-out.

"We don't have the time." Well, are your priorities in order? Are you being a good steward of your time?

> WHEN GOD IS IN THE MIX, YOUR SMALL RESOURCES ARE ENOUGH BECAUSE HE'S THE GOD OF MORE THAN ENOUGH.

You don't need big resources to do something big for God. When God is in the mix, your small resources are enough because He's the God of more than enough. When we have a lot of resources, we don't need to rely on God. We rely on our resources. Stop looking at what you don't have and start using what you do have for the glory of God.

Father wants you just to take what you have, look to Him, give thanks, and then take a step of faith as you walk in obedience. Don't despise small beginnings (see Zechariah 4:10), and don't be overwhelmed by the immensity of the task. Don't let the small size of your resources, the large size of your storm, the depth of your pit, or the gravity of your perceived mistakes hold you back. Father has an assignment with your name on it for His glory!

As we focus on bringing hope to the hopeless, we will be satisfied and fulfilled in Christ. Did you know that you have what it takes for someone else to receive his miracle? Today, Joy Ministries has adopted twelve neighborhoods that are low-income, subsidized housing areas. We have adopted these residents as our own, and we hold outreaches on their turf in order to reach them for Christ. It all started with one step of obedience to go into a single needy neighborhood with a bag of groceries and the message of salvation.

I was amazed to find out that although I didn't have a lot of finances, I had what it took for people to receive their miracles—the miracle of salvation, the miracle of healing, and even the miraculous provision of a bag of groceries.

When we started our back-to-school outreach years ago, I found out that thousands of inner-city children in our community didn't have back-to-school clothes or supplies. Each year, by providing more than 2,000 children with back-to-school necessities, we show them that God cares about their needs and is able to give them their miracles. For many children, owning their own backpacks is a dream come true—a real miracle for those who have never owned one.

Begin with Small Investments of Time and Energy

Even a small investment of time can make a huge difference in the lives of those around us. Every time I invest in the lives of young people through our various outreaches, I'm reminded how my life was changed as a result of people taking the time to meet a vital need in my life just when I needed it most! I frequently tell our staff and volunteers that if they have just one hour a week, they can change a life. There are so many children today who need love, attention, and that ray of hope, just like I did.

Climbing Upward Together

Our goal should be to win souls and then help those individuals continually climb to the next level in God. Father wants all of us to ascend to the next level of faith, the next level in the fruit of the Spirit, and the next level of God's anointing. His desire is to see all of us climb to the next level of boldness and confidence in Christ, the next level of our businesses and ministries, and the next level of blessing in every area of our lives.

Take Possession of the Land

> After the death of Moses the servant of the LORD, the LORD said to Joshua son of Nun, Moses' aide: "Moses my servant is dead. Now then, you and all these people, get ready to cross the Jordan River into the land I am about to give to them—to the Israelites."...So Joshua ordered the officers of the people: "Go through the camp and tell the people, 'Get your supplies ready. Three days from now you will cross the Jordan here to go in and take possession of the land the LORD your God is giving you for your own.'"   (Joshua 1:1–2, 10–11)

We don't climb out of the pit and take possession of the land by sitting back and twiddling our thumbs. We don't advance by lying in bed eating donuts and watching cartoons. We advance by force, and that takes some elbow grease.

Only forceful men and women will lay hold of all that God has for them—those who are forceful against the kingdom of darkness and forceful to advance the kingdom of God. (See Matthew 11:12.) Before we possess anything, we have to take a step of faith. To advance forcefully takes faith—one step at a time.

Lead the People around You

The Lord said to Joshua, "I will give you every place where you set your foot, as I promised Moses" (Joshua 1:3). To receive the places promised to him, Joshua had to set his foot—he had to take an upward step of faith toward the next level. A few verses later, the Lord told Joshua, "Be strong and courageous, because you will lead these people to inherit the land I swore to their forefathers to give them" (verse 6).

I can image that one of Joshua's first thoughts was, *Who, me?* Yes, God wants to use each of us. We are all called to be leaders of the people. Maybe you are called to be a mother. If so, you are a leader, leading your children. If you work at the grocery store, you are a leader. Lead the people who come through your grocery line to Christ.

You were called for such a time as this. (See Esther 4:14.) Don't allow yourself to be intimidated or discouraged, but climb to the next level by praying, by knowing and recognizing the schemes of the enemy, and by focusing forward. When you focus forward, you don't look back. You release yesterday and yesteryear. And, once you've escaped your pit and ascended the peak, make sure to reach out and pull others out of their pits. Then, you will glory together in God's faithfulness!

The Sun Will Shine Again

Although weeping may endure for a night, joy *always* comes in the morning. (See Psalm 30:5 NKJV.) No matter how severe the storm, no matter how deep the pit, no matter how long the night may seem, the sun always shines again. When we remain obedient to Father, He not only brings us out of the pit and into the sunshine, but He also causes His Son to shine through us.

> FATHER NOT ONLY BRINGS US OUT OF THE PIT AND INTO THE SUNSHINE, BUT HE ALSO CAUSES HIS SON TO SHINE THROUGH US.

I can say from experience that no matter how bad the storm, there's always an "after"—a glorious after that includes a beautiful new day. Celebrate the new day. Celebrate the new season. Focus forward and don't look back. Be distraction proof as you release the old and embrace the new. Remember, tough times don't last, but tough people do. If you're in a pit, the palace is not far off!

Chapter Eighteen: Climbing to the Next Level

Points to Ponder

1. In the book of Nehemiah, God's people were in a pit of despair. What did Nehemiah go to rebuild, and why was this important?

2. What can you do to help to rebuild the walls of strength, support, and stability in the lives of others?

3. What qualifies and equips you for this task?

4. Define *process* (as discussed in this chapter) and explain why it is something vital for every one of us to undergo.

5. Has the message of this book given you hope that you can get out of your pit? What choices will you act on today to make your hope a reality?

Meditate on these Scriptures, speak them aloud, and commit them to memory.

So do not throw away your confidence; it will be richly rewarded. You need to persevere so that when you have done the will of God, you will receive what he has promised. (Hebrews 10:35–36)

Consider it pure joy, my brothers, whenever you face trials of many kinds, because you know that the testing of your faith develops perseverance. Perseverance must finish its work so that you may be mature and complete, not lacking anything. (James 1:2–4)

May the God of peace, who through the blood of the eternal covenant brought back from the dead our Lord Jesus, that great Shepherd of the sheep, equip you with everything good for doing his will, and may he work in us what is pleasing to him, through Jesus Christ, to whom be glory for ever and ever. (Hebrews 13:20–21)

This is how we know what love is: Jesus Christ laid down his life for us. And we ought to lay down our lives for our brothers. If anyone has material possessions and sees his brother in need but has no pity on him, how can the love of God be in him? Dear children, let us not love with words or tongue but with actions and in truth. (1 John 3:16–18)